P9-DHJ-306

Praise for

The Road to Success Goes Through the Salad Bar

"Like *The Office* and *Dilbert*, Greg Schwem has the rare ability to make corporate America chuckle at itself. You might not agree with what he has to say about today's business practices and procedures, but I guarantee you will laugh. A smart, fun read."

— Daniel H. Pink, author of *To Sell Is Human* and *Drive*

"Witty, irreverent, funny and spot on! You'll laugh, learn and become wiser as a result of Greg's remarkable insights. This is a must read!"

— Jason Jennings, NY Times bestselling author of *Think BIG-Act Small, Less Is More* and *The Reinventors*

"Greg is a star. His view of the corporate world will leave you smiling."

— Dominick Domasky, author of *Don't Double Bread the Fish*

The Road to Success Goes Through the Salad Bar

A Pile of BS (Business Stories) From a Corporate Comedian

By Greg Schwem

Motivational **PRESS**®

LEADERS IN GLOBAL PUBLISHING

Published by Motivational Press, Inc.
1777 Aurora Road
Melbourne, Florida, 32935
www.MotivationalPress.com

Copyright 2015 © by Greg Schwem

All Rights Reserved

No part of this book may be reproduced or transmitted in any form by any means: graphic, electronic, or mechanical, including photocopying, recording, taping or by any information storage or retrieval system without permission, in writing, from the authors, except for the inclusion of brief quotations in a review, article, book, or academic paper. The authors and publisher of this book and the associated materials have used their best efforts in preparing this material. The authors and publisher make no representations or warranties with respect to accuracy, applicability, fitness or completeness of the contents of this material. They disclaim any warranties expressed or implied, merchantability, or fitness for any particular purpose. The authors and publisher shall in no event be held liable for any loss or other damages, including but not limited to special, incidental, consequential, or other damages. If you have any questions or concerns, the advice of a competent professional should be sought.

Manufactured in the United States of America.

ISBN: 978-1-62865-225-3

Contents

Author's Note

THIS BOOK IS A WORK OF SATIRE. ACCORDING TO MERRIAM-WEBSTER dictionary that means it's, "a literary work holding up human vices and follies to ridicule or scorn." I prefer a simpler definition, "a book that makes you laugh as you're reading it."

This book is not intended to upset or offend any person, company, institution, or law firm that might consider suing me because "all the partners read it and none of us are laughing right now, funny boy." Many of the scenarios depicted within these pages are based on actual events, but involve a little "truth stretching," which falls under the "satire" category. (Honestly your Honor, it does!)

I have painstakingly researched this book meaning I resorted to Wikipedia whenever I had a question. And since ANYBODY can post entries on Wikipedia.org, any factual errors should not be blamed on me, but on society as a whole. Historical dates and time references are accurate, but what I claim happened on those dates may be slightly fictitious. On some pages you will see footnotes pointing to websites where I obtained statistics, figures, and excruciatingly long numbers. I thought it necessary to include footnotes because, after more than 20 years of using Microsoft Word, I realized I had never used the "Insert Footnote" feature. Try it sometime. It gives your work credibility and makes it appear you spent hours in a public library, poring over reference materials. In reality, I wrote most of this book in airport courtesy lounges while the airline attempted to "locate a crew" for my delayed flights. Wait, I think they just arrived.

A few thank yous are in order. First, thanks to my wife, Sue, and daughters, Natalie and Amy, for putting up with the numerous business trips necessary to complete this book. True, I no longer arrive home with armloads full of presents, but I think I've exhausted the supply of trinkets found in airport gift shops. (I hope you enjoyed all those John Grisham novels I purchased. And the snow globes.) I love you all.

Thanks to Paul Crisanti for his photography skills, Laura Swalec for her amazing graphic design work, Justin Sachs and the entire Motivational Press team for taking a chance on this book, and Rob Weisbach for letting me pester him for advice. Also, thanks to Dan Young at Thrivent Financial for generating the idea behind the book's title. I will never look at salad bars the same way again.

Finally, thanks to every corporation, CEO, head of marketing, sales VP, director of Human Resources and assorted other company employees who inadvertently found their way into this book. Yes I've spent years poking fun at your organizations, your cultures, your mission statements, and the "glossary of terms" on your websites (Thanks CenturyLink for informing me that "Data Communication Equipment" is defined as "the equipment required to establish data communication.") But I've met a lot of hard working individuals along the way who arise every morning and head to the office determined to make a difference, while also providing for their families. You are to be commended.

Now please turn off your iPhones, grab a comfortable seat, and spend a few minutes laughing at the crazy world of corporate America. And please share this book with everyone except your legal team.

It's Just Business

Let's get one thing straight: I am not a businessman. I am also not a business person, business individual, daily commuter, telecommuter, venture capitalist, or gray flannel suit. I include that last descriptive phrase only because it appeared when I Googled "businessman synonyms." I don't even own a gray flannel suit, but guess I should purchase one in the event I decide to interview for a job in the business world. My prospective employer will stare across the desk at me—check that, he'll stare at a computer screen since all job interviews are now conducted via Skype—and think, "Wow, we need this guy. Look at that suit!"

Other businessman synonyms that do not apply to me are "baron," "capitalist," "financier," "industrialist," and "trafficker." I'd happily put any of these next to my name except trafficker, which sounds illegal[1].

Kids, have fun trick or treating tonight. Just stay away from the trafficker at the end of the block.

I am a "business owner" because I meet the requirements: I own a business. However, my firm, (I like that word), contains exactly one employee: me. That makes me, "self-employed," a term I disdain because

---

1   Except in states that have legalized marijuana. Then it sounds impressive

it gives the impression no one would hire me. Saying you are "self-employed" makes you sound like the kid in college who started his own fraternity after every house on campus rejected him.[2]

The most important requirement of a self-employed individual is giving the appearance that he or she presides over an international conglomerate with thousands of employees. The easiest, and cheapest, way to do this is to include a menu function in your phone greeting. Callers who contact my office hear, "For a staff directory, press one" followed by, "Please spell the person's first and last name." Of course everybody is spelling my name, but they don't need to know that, do they?

Just as I am not affiliated with business, I am also not a "corporate" individual. I do not work in corporate America; I'm not a cog in the corporate wheel nor have I ever climbed the corporate ladder. Incidentally, where is this "ladder" I hear so much about? I have walked through numerous company headquarters and have yet to see an apparatus in the lobby featuring employees firmly gripping various rungs.[3] Now THAT would be an excellent conversation piece.

What's that?

That's our corporate ladder. Joe just needs to mount three more steps and he'll become s VP of marketing.

Who's on the rung above him?

That's Bill. He's been blocking Joe's path for the last four years.

I have no background in the business world, have never worked in the aforementioned world, and rarely read the business page in my local newspaper unless I spot a headline that has something to do with Apple stock. Then I read the article and think, "Wow, if I had purchased Apple back in 1980, I might be a tycoon by now. And an industrialist."[4]

Now let's quickly recap since, if you are a typical book reader, you have

---

2 That wasn't me. I received one, possibly two fraternity invitations

3 Rumor has it, some Silicon Valley firms are installing them

4 A $5,000 investment in Apple's 1980 IPO was worth $1.3 million in 2014. How you feeling now?

retained nothing so far. Most likely this is because, while reading, you are simultaneously texting friends and checking Fantasy Football stats. I have ZERO business education, ZERO business background, and have worked in ZERO actual businesses. Which makes me perfectly qualified to author a book on business. Seriously, do you think our nation's elected officials have any knowledge of contagious diseases when they allocate 50 million dollars to fight the Ebola plague? Of course not. That's why, as you half-attentively read this book, think of me as a "congressional expert" in the world of business.

My dad was a businessman. Actually, when I was very young and asked what Daddy did all day, he and my mother responded, "Daddy makes money," while hoping I would drop the inquisition and go play with Legos so they could resume drinking highballs in peace. I interpreted "makes money" to mean Daddy sat at a workbench from 9 a.m. to 5 p.m., drawing five dollar bills by hand and shaping precious metals into what would eventually become pennies and nickels. Looking back I realize, "Daddy makes money," was far easier for a five year old to comprehend than, "Daddy sells 30-year term life policies and whole life annuities, which can be converted into one lump sum payment if the buyer so chooses."

As I grew older, I realized that being a businessman meant putting on a coat and tie, (or a gray flannel suit if you were really serious), leaving the house every morning, and returning home each evening. Those eight hours in between were spent, "conducting business." Occasionally my dad didn't return home, which meant he was "away on business," "traveling for business," or "missing and please contact the local police department." His seat at the dinner table sat empty while my mother, sister, and I ate meals undoubtedly paid for with the money dad had already made. We talked little, saving conversations for when Dad returned from his "business trip."

The word "business" can be applied in so many situations. In social settings we've all been told to stay out of someone else's business or worse, mind our own business. The latter phrase includes profanity if used at a youth sporting event.

IRATE PARENT 1: "C'mon ref. Number 19 is throwing elbows. That's a yellow card!"

PARENT OF NUMBER 19: She's not doing a thing.

IRATE PARENT 1: Mind your own &#$#@ business!

IRATE PARENT 2: You tell 'em Donna!

When we annoy or trump another individual, we are "giving them the business." When we get serious about a particular task or issue, we "mean business." We groggily take our dogs outside at 2:30 a.m. so they can "do their business." When we screw somebody over or worse, get screwed ourselves, we shrug it off, saying, "It's just business." None of these clichés have anything to do with my Dad going to an office each morning; they simply add to the mystery surrounding this strange phenomenon known as "business."

When I entered college, I realized "business" was also a major and a possible career, albeit very broad in scope. Those majoring in "business" basically wore signs around their necks saying, "I have no idea what I actually want to do after receiving a diploma."[5] Business majors were silently snickered at by the rest of the student body, even those majoring in "communications," a practice that exists to this day.

Don't believe me? Line up five college students and ask them their majors. You might hear "Molecular Biology, Occupational Therapy, Art History, Journalism, and Business." See what I mean? "Business" is so non-descript, so vague. Majoring in business could be one's way of saying, "I want to create the next social media empire" or "I want to be 'Barista of the Day' at my local Starbucks, a place I should be able to work since I possess a business degree."[6]

The only way to be taken seriously as a business major is to become

---

5   Unless a company needs an employee who can shotgun a Budweiser

6   A business degree plus a graduate degree should get you off the weekend shift at Starbucks

a double major unless, of course, that second major is communications. A business/communications major is telling the world, "I will not have a job when I exit college but my communications degree will allow me to concisely explain why I am unemployed."

And yet surprisingly, business majors eventually find work and become real live businessmen and businesswomen. Perhaps it's because having a business degree allows its owner to walk into any building where people appear to be working, ask, "Are you running a business here?", and then say, "Great, I'm qualified. Here is my degree."

There are many ways to enter the business world. The most common is to take an entry level job at an existing business, work diligently for approximately 17 minutes, and then quit upon realizing that Snapchatting with your boyfriend is frowned upon during weekly staff meetings. Or quit after making the shocking discovery that the employee cafeteria only serves sushi on Thursdays. U.S. Bureau of Labor statistics reveal the average Millennial, (born between 1977 and 1997), had changed jobs six times between 18 and 26.[7] Furthermore, they switch jobs once every three years.[8] If you are reading this book at your business and see a Millennial who has been on the job for over three years, walk over and take a subtle, over-the-shoulder glance at his or her computer screen. Chances are it will contain either a resume or a job search website.

"Job hopping," as it is typically called, is not a new phenomenon although it is perceived as one. Back in the post—World War II era, when American business began to boom, employees often spent their entire careers at one business. They entered the building fresh faced in 1950 and emerged 37 years later, retired and respected by their peers, at least publically. Privately their peers breathed sighs of relief and thought, "Geez, I didn't think Stan was ever going to leave. How old is that guy? Like 115?"

---

7   http://www.bls.gov/news.release/nlsyth.nr0.htm

8   http://www.forbes.com/sites/jeannemeister/2012/08/14/job-hopping-is-the-new-normal-for-millennials-three-ways-to-prevent-a-human-resource-nightmare/

But Labor Bureau statistics show that the youngest Baby Boomers, (a polite description for "people who have actually used a rotary phone"), had an average of 11 jobs[9] by the time they reached their 40s, proving what all federally funded studies eventually conclude: Nobody is ever happy and nobody ever will be happy.

The easiest way to avoid becoming trapped in an unfulfilling job is to start one's own business. Again, times have changed when it comes to actually succeeding at this. In the 1950s, it involved finding a vacant building and hanging a sign which included the owner's name, signifying that yes, this person owns this business. "Jack's Furniture," "Orville's Appliances," and "Vinny's Bail Bonds" were examples of businesses created by a single individual. Today starting a business means launching a website and then watching YouTube videos while waiting for somebody to actually visit the site. Those who pile up millions of web hits typically go on to become business "magnates." Those whose website traffic consists of immediate family members are deemed business "failures" and go on to try other businesses vowing that, this time around, the website will be truly awesome.

There is also the option of starting a business WITH a family member. Some of the world's most profitable companies are family owned including Wal-Mart, Ford Motor Company, and Comcast. A family owned business that actually succeeds is shocking simply because the average family cannot even spend Thanksgiving Day together without threats of physical violence. And yet, siblings are supposed to work side by side continuously? Come on! Ford Motor Company is successful only because members of the Ford clan work at opposite ends of the assembly line.

Even the act of naming a business will generate an argument when family members decide to become partners:

Let's call it Steve and Bill's Car Wash.

---

9   http://www.bls.gov/news.release/pdf/nlsoy.pdf

Why not Bill and Steve's Car Wash?

Because I'm older.

But I came up with the idea. And I paid for the sponges.

I paid for the hoses.

And you know where you can stick those hoses?

Inevitably these disagreements lead to lawsuits or worse, competition. A classic example is the case of Manganaro's Grosseria Italiana which, prior to its closing in 2012, operated on Ninth Avenue in New York City for over a century. In 1956, Manganaro family members, buoyed by their success, decided to expand and open a sandwich shop, Manganaro's Hero Boy, next door. Then the fireworks began. A dispute over who had naming rights to its most popular creation, the Hero-Boy sandwich, erupted. Lawsuits were filed and family members didn't speak to one another even though the businesses continued operating side by side. I never patronized the Hero Boy shop, but often included it when making food recommendations to friends visiting New York City.

"You have to try Manganaro's."

"What if we don't like it?"

"Then go next door...to Manganaro's."

Families that do get along pass businesses down through generations. Sam Walton's son, Rob, is now chairman of Wal-Mart's Board of Directors while William Clay Ford Jr., the great grandson of auto magnate Henry Ford, steers the car giant bearing his name. In June 2015 Rupert Murdoch handed control of 21st Century Fox to his son James, who vowed to carry on his dad's legacy by putting out a nightly mix of lies, errors and one sided reporting known as FOX News.

Also, if you're male and your dad owns a funeral home, by law you must succeed him in the dead body business. Have you ever seen a funeral home that doesn't include the phrase, "And Sons," in the title? Are women forbidden from becoming funeral directors? I haven't been to an abundance of funerals, but guarantee I have never paid condolences at William M. Smith and Daughters funeral home.

When I graduated Northwestern University, my Dad had abandoned the insurance "business" for the electronic manufacturer's representative "business." Although I majored in journalism, it was his dream, like all Dads, for his son to "join the business." My journalism degree, he assumed, would help me write eloquent, yet threatening letters asking delinquent customers to pay up.

One day I accompanied him on sales calls so he could "show me the business." That day consisted of me following him into various warehouses and meeting engineers with the social skills of a hibernating grizzly bear. While I stood idly by, the engineers and my Dad discussed whether it was more beneficial to employ through-hole or surface-mount construction on a printed circuit board and whether components should be attached via bulk wave soldering or reflow ovens. I was impressed with my Dad's purported knowledge of these foreign topics, but by midafternoon, I realized he was faking it through a series of head nods and generic phrases like, "I agree with whatever you guys think is best."

"Well Russ, we think the circuit boards would be more durable if we urinated on them."

"That works for me. By the way, my commission is 20 percent."

At day's end, my dad turned to me and said, "What do you think of the business?"

I asked if he would consider opening a car wash with me.

Instead, I used my degree, actually becoming a real working journalist, first at a South Florida newspaper and then at WPTV, an NBC-affiliated TV station in the same market. The newspaper had an actual business section, led by a business editor who funneled stories to a team of business reporters. The only time I actually conversed with the business editor was during March, as it was he who organized the office NCAA tournament basketball pool. Incidentally, what started as a harmless little game of choosing which teams would beat other teams over a three week period has become "big business."

While at the newspaper, I was the crime reporter, spending my days covering homicides and drug deals conducted in stifling temperatures. If I were a South Florida drug dealer, I would wait until a cool breeze wafted in from the Atlantic Ocean before dropping off my supply. I once saw 500 kilos of confiscated cocaine and it looked far too heavy and cumbersome to lift in 95 percent humidity.

Rarely did the worlds of crime and business overlap, but when they did, I was forced to hand the story to the business section in spite of my pleas to write it myself.

ME: Boss, the police just discovered 10 dead bodies, shot execution style, in a crack house. How about I write a story on the effect that might have on South Florida tourism?

EDITOR: That sounds more like a story for the business section.

When I defected to the television station, I reported on every subject, business included. Unlike the world of newspapers, TV reporters don't have specific "beats." At 9 a.m., we dash to the local zoo because a baby ostrich is about to be born; at 11 a.m., we race into a school board meeting just in time for an impending vote that, if approved, would make the entire district "peanut product free;" at 3 p.m., we cover a multi-car interstate pileup that we most likely caused because we were speeding to our next assignment. At 6 p.m., we go on the air live and try not to mix up the stories we just covered.

Today, three people were killed on Interstate 95, apparently after having fatal allergic reactions to peanut butter cookies. The sole survivor was this adorable baby ostrich!

On October 19, 1987, I was thrust into covering the most important business story of my career. On that day, the stock market plunged 508 points, earning it the title, "Black Monday," a label that would hold until Sept. 16, 2008 when a similar crash became known as "Blacker Monday."

Currently a team of graduate students at the Wharton School of Business is learning how to make irresponsible, risky financial decisions that, in 2023, will result in "Blackest Monday," accompanied by a market drop of 3,739 points. This is why I keep $500 in small bills rolled up in my mattress. I suggest you do the same.

I knew nothing about the stock market in 1987, seeing that my investment portfolio consisted of clipping laundry detergent coupons from the Sunday paper. But I did play tennis with a real live stockbroker, a fact I casually mentioned to the news director that bleak October morning.

"Go interview him," he commanded.

"What should I ask him?"

"How should I know? I'm only the news director!"

Cameraman in tow, I entered my friend's office where I found him simultaneously staring at three computer screens, the look on his face alternating between panic and resignation. Thrusting a microphone towards his lips, I posed the most technical, hard-hitting business question I could think of:

"Are you free for doubles this Saturday?"

He continued staring at the screens while answering subsequent questions about the crash and what it might entail for the average individual. The answer to that question is "nothing" for the average individual does not own stock. Stock market crashes only affect those who own more than one Maserati. Unable to grasp the severity of the situation, I instead focused on my friend's demeanor. He was aloof, even rude as he never made eye contact with me, choosing instead to gaze catatonically at mountains of information flashing across the screens, often interrupting me to hit "refresh." Today this behavior is called "being a teenager."

I'm sure my mind was elsewhere too since I most likely had a show that evening. While in Florida, I pursued my first love of standup comedy.

Okay, I loved covering murders too, but I'm in that small category of sick individuals who enjoy seeing a supine form laying in the middle of a street, surrounded by yellow tape while a group of crime scene technicians works frantically to do – well, nothing since the person is already dead. Crime scene technician may be the only job left where speed is not a requirement. Eventually I decided it was more fun to make people laugh than to enter their living rooms via a small screen during the dinner hour and inform them that a mass murderer was living in their neighborhood—specifically in their child's treehouse— and we had EXCLUSIVE video to prove it. I became a full time standup comedian, quitting my TV reporting job approximately two and a half years after quitting my newspaper job. So, if you're keeping score, I'd had three jobs by age 26, putting me squarely in the norm of Labor Department statistics.

Today I'm a "business humorist." I was formerly a "corporate standup comedian," but dropped that title after hearing potential clients talk about their past experiences with comedians.

"We had a comedian at our sales conference a few years ago. We specifically told him, 'no profanity' and he dropped 17 f-bombs in the first five minutes."

"You don't have to worry about that with me," I'll reply. "I'm not a comedian, I'm a business humorist."

"Really?"

"F--k yeah. I mean, yeah."

In a nutshell, I travel the country, (and occasionally the world), making fun of business, a topic that spawns a wealth of material. In the business world, we hold daily meetings, agreeing after two hours in a conference room to "meet again." We discuss business via conference calls while a dog barks in the background because one participant is phoning in from his home office. We check our office email at 2:30 a.m. while in the midst of that long overdue vacation we desperately needed because we had to get away from the office. Every morning we enter the office through a secure set of glass partitions, which magically disappear when we "swipe in," using a plastic security card we clip to our clothing. We use the clip so we don't lose the card. Face it, our security cards are the equivalent of mittens we clipped to our coats when we were five years old.

I didn't set out to be a business humorist. Like all novice comedians, my goal was simple: Work comedy clubs, get discovered by an agent, move to California, land my own sitcom, and spend the rest of my career riding around in a private jet that would shuttle me to Vegas appearances five times a year and Monterey, California once a year where I would tee off in the Pebble Beach Celebrity Pro-Am and miss the cut alongside Clint Eastwood.

But I was fortunate to be working comedy clubs in the early 1990s, when home computers and the Technology Age in general were in their infancy, but about to explode. Remember Windows 95? Many people erroneously think the "95" referred to the year the operating system was launched.[10] In reality 95 represented the number of hours spent waiting in line to purchase a PC containing the Windows 95 operating system, and then the number of hours spent on hold before a Microsoft technical support representative answered the phone and told you that, unfortunately, Windows 95 was now obsolete.

I wrote material about technology, inserted it into my nightclub act and, before long, was performing at holiday office parties and golf outings. I supplemented my standup income by becoming a tradeshow presenter, trying to entertain business people in five-to seven-minute spurts while informing them that yes, the new Compaq PC has THREE ISA slots, which is way better than TWO ISA slots, even though nobody has ever figured out what to do with ONE ISA slot.

My tradeshow background lead to appearances at sales conferences, product launches, awards banquets, and other venues where hard working business people needed a good laugh. The coolest venue? The 19,000 seat

---

10   August 24, 1995 to be exact

Bradley Center in Milwaukee. Granted it was filled with Northwestern Mutual insurance agents, but even they know how to party.

The strangest location? The bowels of a Catamaran sailing around San Diego harbor. Ten software employees sat in a circle while I stood in the middle and tried to make them laugh about the software business for...45 minutes! Those were my instructions from the CEO: "Do about 45." After seeing the set up, I asked if he meant 45 minutes or seconds.

Today, when a business person asks what I do, I reply, "I'm a business humorist." When they ask me to elaborate, I reply, "I get paid to say what you wish you could say." It's a strange way to make a living but for me, it's good business.

And it doesn't even require a gray flannel suit.

II

The Road to Success Goes Through the Salad Bar

CRAIGSLIST POST, CIRCA EARLY-19TH CENTURY

Man seeking men: *Strong, able-bodied Englishman seeks those of similar build to attack factories and protest technological advancements. We call ourselves "Luddites" and we will not stand idly by as machinery replaces our skills. Join our movement. The plusses? Higher wages for our services. The minuses? Clashes with British armed forces and possible executions. Next meeting is this Tuesday. Transportation provided via horse-drawn wagon. NOTE: Do not arrive via steam-powered vessel; remember we are PROTESTING technology, not taking advantage of it.*

Historians point to the Industrial Revolution, beginning around 1760, as the event ushering in the concept of steady hiring, leading to business formation. For reasons that remain unknown to this day, British farmers, who had been breathing clean air in spacious countryside environments while setting their own hours and work attire, flocked to cities for jobs that involved toiling 10 to 14 hour days in horrific conditions, six days a week, with no casual attire Friday or cafeterias serving complimentary kale smoothies. This en masse migration was caused by "factories," humungous buildings in Great Britain that sprang up literally overnight, churning out everything from steel to paper to textiles. After explaining to nearby residents what a textile was—"It's something you wear...and your great great great grandkids will wear just enough of it to cover their private areas—" these factories commenced operation, making strange noises and emitting noxious fumes into the heavens. Factory owners realized that, in order to continue polluting the atmosphere 24 hours a day, they would need machine operators. The operators, in turn, needed foremen to instruct them in the finer art of running the machines, seeing that online technical support was still hundreds of years away. The foremen needed executives to purchase the smoke wielding machines even though none had any idea what they were buying.

Does smoke come out of it?

Absolutely. It can produce white, black or gray smoke 24 hours a day. The world's cardinals can convene here the next time they choose a pope.

We don't need a pope. Can it produce a textile?

I think so.

Fantastic. Where do I sign?

Suddenly any able-bodied male between the ages of 7 and 91 could easily find a job, no questions asked. Women still weren't part of the workforce during the Industrial Revolution. Most stayed home, spending long hours futilely attempting to wash the smoke smell out of their husband's clothes. Were the Industrial Revolution occurring today, those same women would band together and create a reality show entitled *Real Factory Housewives of the Revolution.* Thankfully this was not the case in the 18th century.

The work their husbands did was incredibly dangerous; occasionally factory executives had the unpleasant task of knocking on a wife's door and grimly informing her that this new age of steam powered machinery had its drawbacks. Failing to get out of the way of a steam powered locomotive for example.

There were naysayers to this new way of doing business. The Luddites, comprised of skilled textile workers who had the unfortunate distinction of watching their jobs replaced by spinning frames and power looms, sought to destroy those machines and, in some cases, succeeded. Legend has it the Luddites were led by Ned Ludd, who smashed two stocking frames in 1779 after waiting on hold over three hours with stocking frame support staff. Luddites were eventually rounded up and sentenced to hard labor, meaning they got their old jobs back.

In spite of this highly unregulated environment, where only the wealthiest controlled the factories, the Industrial Revolution eventually spread to Western Europe and the American colonies, which desperately sought independence from Great Britain and a chance to create their own hazardous working conditions. Until then, everybody living in the colonies turned to Ben Franklin for advice. When he wasn't helping draft historical documents, this mild-mannered, portly gentleman was churning out inventions faster than Donald Trump churns out self-aggrandizing press releases. Among Franklin's contributions to society: bifocals, a stove/fireplace, a lightning rod, a urinary catheter, and a first generation iPod. Steve Jobs would merely modify the design centuries later.

The Industrial Revolution ended in approximately 1820 after workers, realizing they hadn't had a vacation in 60 years, walked off their jobs and went on a Jamaican cruise. Even though the revolution was over, it transformed not only the job market, but also lead to the rise of urban environments or "cities." The "cities," in turn, would later give rise to all the features of city living including, "90-minute commutes," "muggings," and "drive by shootings."

The second en masse employment event was The New Deal, a term coined by Franklin Delano Roosevelt, also known as "the first president with a text message-friendly name." (JFK and LBJ would follow in FDR's footsteps). This monumental event occurred shortly after the Depression, a dark time in American history when banks failed, the stock market crashed, and millionaires were forced to sell apples on the street to make ends meet. A similar Depression occurred in 2007-09, but with slightly less dire consequences. In that case, millionaires were forced to sell one of their three boats and at least consider the idea of temporarily subletting their New York penthouses. Economists agree that depressions and recessions are byproducts of the American economy and will occur sporadically until somebody realizes how easy it is for a Goldman Sachs intern to manipulate the stock market simply by pressing the "Shift L" key. Also, depressions don't last forever. By June 2014, the American economy had regained the 8.7 million jobs it lost in the last Depression, never mind that the most popular job in June 2014 was "joint roller at Denver-area marijuana dispensary."

The New Deal was FDR's way of saying, "I am at least thinking of ways this country can work. Of course, I'm not thinking too hard because, as President of the United States, I already have a job." But Roosevelt and his cabinet members put their heads together and decided Americans needed to be put back to work and needed better working conditions once they had obtained employment. Frances Perkins, Roosevelt's secretary of labor, envisioned a work force with a 40-hour workweek, a minimum wage, worker and unemployment compensation, a federal law banning child labor, direct federal aid for unemployment relief, Social Security, and health insurance. Years later all of these benefits would be scrapped for anyone choosing to work at Wal-Mart.

To help the unemployed find jobs, Roosevelt and his cabinet created the Public Works Administration, which immediately decided all the machines built during the Industrial Revolution no longer worked and needed to be dismantled and sold for scrap metal. On a good day, this brought in considerably more income than apple sales. The PWA thrived on government funds allocated to construct government buildings, airports, hospitals, schools, roads, bridges, and dams. Suddenly there were jobs galore, even though most able-bodied American workers hadn't the slightest idea how to build a road, bridge, or dam. But Roosevelt, being the forward thinker that he was, knew that hiring unskilled laborers to connect diverse geographical areas would lead to future generations of employment for road construction workers hired to fix the cracks, potholes, and other shoddy workmanship left behind by New Deal workers.

President Barack Obama was also fond of trumpeting the, "let's put Americans back to work by building roads and bridges," battle cry during his Depression. Exactly one bridge was actually constructed during the Obama administration; a structure over a coin-filled fountain that connected two anchor stores at a Yuma, Arizona mall. Seven workers built it in three days despite more than one million dollars in cost overruns. [11]

In 1941, when the U.S entered World War II and men went off to battle, women became an integral part of the work force. That's right guys, it was those cute, lovable gals who manufactured all of war's necessary components, including uniforms, backpacks, and bombs capable of wiping out entire cities in seconds. Women who manufactured the latter were never told what they were creating and never questioned why other women could wear skirts to the office while they donned hazmat suits and nitrile rubber gloves.

When the war ended, many feared a slowdown in military spending would plunge the country back into another depression. But President Dwight David Eisenhower, (not DDE), decided he liked having at least a couple of weapons of mass destruction available in several strategic locations—in underground bunkers, at the golf course and beneath his desk to name a few—so the military industrial complex, as it was known, continued. Plus, we could always make bombs for smaller countries about to start their own wars, a practice that continues to this day.

---

11   Coins from the fountain were retrieved and used to pay the overruns

---

Meanwhile, the employment landscape was changing yet again. Horny American soldiers, fresh off years spent living in military barracks overseas, returned to this country and had sex with any female who dared glance their way. The ensuing Baby Boom meant men had responsibilities; they needed homes to live in, cars for their office commutes, taverns to stop at on the way home from the office, and shopping centers to provide goods for the children they were siring every nine months. The construction and automotive industries exploded. Office buildings sprang up, ushering in the modern business era which exists today, except that kale smoothies still weren't available until 2012. Also business owners became more picky in who they hired, meaning potential applicants had to at least demonstrate the ability to read, write, and speak in complete sentences. The federal government hired workers possessing none of those traits.

The job application has undergone several transformations since its inception. In the 1960s, applicants were instructed to sit in smoke filled waiting rooms and place personal information into corresponding boxes. A written essay, usually entitled, "What I can bring to this organization?" was next and required well thought out sentences that could easily be the difference between employment and rejection. All of the responses were carefully read by employers and all information submitted by applicants was 100 percent truthful because, in the 1960s, people still had morals.

The 1970s were a carefree time in which recreational drug use and casual sex abounded. Consequently, the job application mirrored those times. In addition to filling out personal information, applicants might have to answer, "If you could be any insect, what would it be and why?" The only incorrect response was, "A 17-year cicada so I wouldn't have to return to this cesspool until 1987."

Work environments mirrored the laidback times as well. Bourbon, gin, and vodka sat in desk drawers alongside paperclips, pens and staplers. It also wasn't uncommon for the typical male office worker to take long lunches featuring two or three martinis, get in a car, drive back to the office, and then spend a few more hours at his desk sleeping until 5 p.m. My dad freely admitted he financed my college education with the help of a few vodka soaked olives and a veal shank with soup, salad, and baked potato, all consumed at 11:30 a.m.

Women wore short skirts, worn even shorter if the woman was seeking a promotion, and always made sure their male counterparts' desks were stocked with a variety of liquor. While they didn't join the men for three martini lunches, they spent the time rifling through the desk drawers, compiling blackmail material.

All of this changed in the 1980s, with the invention of the personal computer, also known as, "the day work stopped being fun." Typewriters, a machine invented solely to make it sound like the user was working, and featuring a metal arm that had to be swatted every time a bell "dinged" so the user could continue writing[12] became extinct. So did the ability to take out your frustrations by angrily pushing the typewriter's carriage return so forcefully that it fell from its hinges. Workers realized it was exorbitantly more expensive and dangerous to take out your frustrations on a keyboard by shoving one's hand through the monitor. Liquor also disappeared from office desks because the expense of spilling Scotch on a keyboard far outweighed the buzz created from drinking one shot.

The other transformation which sucked fun out of the office environment was the rise of the office cubicle, known to new, enthusiastic employees as, "MY cube," and jaded veteran workers as, "this (INSERT NUMEROUS PROFANITIES HERE) cube." Invented in 1960 by Robert Propst, who died in 2000 and, contrary to popular belief, was not beaten to death by disgruntled office workers, the cube became immensely popular in the dot com era. Suddenly employees who were used to retreating into their private offices came into work one Monday and found those offices in the middle of a large room, with only three flimsy metal walls separating them from row upon row of other identical "offices." The metal walls were covered in thin carpeted layers, allowing

---

12   Readers born after 1980, this machine really existed. I swear!

employees to decorate their personal spaces with a few family portraits and at least one cat calendar, but that was it for individuality.

The job application and interview process began to change dramatically in the 1980s as well. True, applicants still had to sit in a, (now smoke free!), environment, filling out applications, and waiting for their names to be called. But once they sat across from their prospective bosses, the questions were more pointed and often oozed with a sense of panic. The most popular question? "Do you know how to operate Microsoft Word and Excel?" If the candidate replied in the affirmative, a typical follow up question was, "Please explain what Microsoft Word and Excel are. I'm the CEO and I have no idea."

By the 1990s, work environments were 100 percent computerized, with so many wires and cables running through ceiling tiles that simply flushing an office toilet could cause a power surge that forced the entire office to shut down while frantic employees tried desperately to locate the one person who could rectify the situation. The IT manager, as he or she came to be known, was usually found at the one working computer, playing World of Warcraft.

The Internet replaced newspaper want ads as the singular tool required to land employment. Job seekers flocked to LinkedIn, also known as "Facebook for non-losers." Users posted resumes complete with PowerPoint presentations, video clips, and brilliantly flowing "work history" prose that was obviously written with help from the Microsoft Thesaurus. "Mid-level manager" magically became "Top tier executive" while "receptionist who answers phones" morphed into "Detail-oriented business analyst with strong problem-solving skills." The average LinkedIn profile also contains at least one self-congratulatory accomplishment. For example, "Assisted in negotiating temporary ceasefire between warring Middle East countries by participating in online Yahoo poll asking if I thought war was a bad thing. I responded 'yes.'"

Company websites also became the "go to" place to find jobs. Rather than walking into a reception area, armed with a resume and a body of work, and asking if jobs were available, job applicants could simply call up a company's website, click "careers," "job openings," or "Want to Work Here?" and see that yes, jobs were available providing the employee met the following qualifications:

» Expertise in UI framework experience, preferably ExtJS using OOP

» The ability to monitor CPU, I/O and JVU performance

» A clear understanding of Oracle R12-OM,IB,SC,AP,AR

» Outstanding verbal skills

» Because today's online job applications do not come with a person sitting across a desk that can answer simple questions like, "What the hell does this job entail?", "Are there health benefits?", and "Do you have an office Christmas party?", the applicant must decipher the verbiage on his or her own. Most companies, before listing available jobs, invite prospective employees to click a link titled, "Why work here?" which lists all the amazing benefits the company has to offer. Eventually, it becomes clear how to translate job vernacular. For example:

» *Work in an environment that embraces individual differences.* It's okay if you're gay, but that doesn't mean employees won't whisper about you when you leave for lunch.

» *We value corporate responsibility.* If you plan to get drunk this weekend, be damn sure nobody is around with a video-enabled cell phone.

» *We're a green company.* You will be mocked mercilessly if you bring a sandwich to work in a non-biodegradable bag. Even the gay employees will disparage you.

» *We have fun!* If your idea of fun is spending your hard earned weekend volunteering at a food pantry or manning a water station at a breast cancer Fun Run at 5 a.m.

If the applicant still decides to pursue employment after reading this list, the next step is to be able to correctly interpret all job requirements:

» *Some travel required.* You will leave for a business trip when your child is three and won't see him again until he graduates college. And that will be done via FaceTime since you'll be in an airport somewhere.

» *Flexible hours.* Your choice. Work nights and weekends or weekends and nights.

» *Ability to lift at least 50 pounds.* Your first job responsibility will be to remove the crate that inadvertently fell on the employee you will be replacing.

» *Spanish fluency preferred.* Not vital, but the inability to understand this language means you will never know what half the workforce is saying about you.

Having read all that, it's time for the job prospect to do in seconds what generations of workers before him had to spend all day doing: Submit the resume. While online applications do indeed save time, and allow unemployed individuals to apply for literally hundreds of jobs in a single day, there is no way to tell where these resumes actually land when the owners click "send." There are three possibilities:

1. A spam folder, where it will reside between "FREE PORN STARRING BARELY LEGAL HOTTIES!" and "GUYS, NEED A LITTLE 'EXTRA' IN THE BEDROOM?"

2. The marketing department, whose director will quickly scan it, searching for ideas that could help the company. If any are found, the director quickly deletes the resume and then proposes identical ideas at the next staff meeting.

3. The desk of a current employee with roughly the same job duties as the applicant. The paranoid employee adds a few items under "past

work experience" such as "Picked up trash during Prison Work Release Program" before forwarding the resume to the Human Resources Director, ensuring that the job prospect is thoroughly unqualified to join the company.

By total accident, the resume could also land in the inbox of the person charged with doing the actual hiring. That person will most likely set up a "phone interview," a grueling 30-second interrogation in which the employer's sole responsibility is to determine whether the job prospect is capable of answering a phone. Phone interviews are easy to master, providing the applicant doesn't get a sudden case of hiccups when the phone rings.

Finally, if the applicant has leaped over these major hurdles, the next step is a face-to-face interview, which, in the age of technology-enabled job applications, means knowing how to operate Skype. Oh, did you think it actually meant personal contact? Shame on you!

Skype was created in 2003 solely to keep home office workers from taking conference calls in their boxer shorts. A webcam, microphone, computer, and lack of modesty are all that is necessary to talk with a prospective employer, even if that employer's office is next door. While Skype seems an impersonal way to communicate, many job candidates use it to their advantage by making sure every Skype interview contains the following elements:

1. A collection of awards in the background. These can range from your college diploma to the "Participation" trophy you earned from your seventh grade swim team. Remember, Skype video is always grainy so an employer will never be able to make out how lame your awards really are.

2. A personal visit from your best-looking child. Halfway through the interview have said child walk into frame. Attire is important; the kid should be decently dressed, (do not clothe him or her in stained overalls that make it appear your saving account balance is $3.85. Remember, you own a PC with a webcam.)

Conversely, do not waltz them in front of the camera wearing the latest Abercrombie & Fitch duds. Doing so gives the impression that you have plenty of money and don't need this job. No need for the child to cry on camera, at least not immediately. A simple hug and then an exit, stage right should do the trick

3. Even the most hardened employer can't resist a dog so have one at the ready, even if you are highly allergic to pet hair. Golden Retriever and Labrador puppies will melt anybody's heart in terms of cuteness, but an underfed Rottweiler or Chow can be equally effective as many companies have been known to hire employees simply out of fear. National Basketball Association owners stock entire teams this way.

Of course, firms seeking the most qualified employees can bypass all this job assistance technology by resorting to a most primitive method of finding the ideal candidate, one created by my friend Dan who works at a large Minnesota insurance firm.

"I just want someone who's creative, can quickly make decisions, knows how to solve problems, works well with others, and has excellent time management skills," he said, when I asked what he valued in a co-worker.

"And you think you can find that person just by looking at resumes?" I replied skeptically. "People do lie on their job applications."

"I realize that. But they can't lie at the salad bar."

"And what exactly does salad have to do with employment? Are you limiting your search to vegans?" I asked.

"Not necessarily. But I can spot all those qualities I rattled off just by inviting candidates to lunch at a salad bar," he said. "And the best part is, they have no idea. They think they're having a meal when, in reality, the way they operate the crouton tongs could be the difference between a career at a major financial planning firm with health benefits—and a part time job at Ramblin' Ray's Burger Emporium."

"That's weird," I said.

"Try it," he said. "The next time you're in line, watch the people in front of you and imagine working with them."

At precisely noon the next day I found myself at my local grocery store's salad bar. I took my place behind an early 20s male, someone I could easily envision pounding the pavement with his resume. Plastic container in tow, he approached the leafy green selections, consisting of iceberg lettuce, spring mix and spinach. He piled all three into the box.

"Hmmm. Shows creativity," I thought.

The vegetables were next. I watched as he dipped the tongs into the cherry tomatoes and removed one, then two, then three, before hesitating and putting one back.

"They're tomatoes, not hand grenades," I mumbled silently, while checking my watch. "Take a few and move. I don't have all day."

Without hesitation, he jammed the tongs deep into the red onions, pulling out a heap and smothering the lettuce.

"A real individualist. Doesn't care what others think of him," I mentally noted, knowing that his pungent onion breath would force co-workers into hiding.

The garbanzo beans, beets, and green peppers received not a flicker of interest.

"Can be aloof and alienating," I thought. "Unwilling to try new ideas."

While adding cottage cheese to his plate, he suddenly whipped out his iPhone and answered a text. The line came to a halt. I huffed loudly. He noticed.

"Sorry," he said. "Want to go ahead of me?"

"No, take your time," I replied, torn between his sense of compassion and lousy multitasking skills.

We were nearing the end. He approached the dressings and toppings where I watched him heap three large ladles of Thousand Island onto his concoction, along with a spoonful each of sesame seeds and Craisins. In spite of the excessive weight, he seemed unfazed by the large number that appeared on the scale.

"Wasteful," I muttered. Could this man be trusted to make sound financial decisions?

"That will be $9.85," the cashier said.

He plopped his Visa on the counter.

"Sorry," the cashier replied. We don't accept credit cards for orders under $10."

"I don't have any cash on me," he said.

"There's an ATM over there," she gestured. "I'll wait since I already rung it up. Better hurry."

"Rude, unprepared, not able to anticipate the unexpected," I said soft, but not too soft.

"Are you talking about me?" he asked.

"No," I lied and watched him trudge to the ATM. Truth be told, I felt sorry for him. Will this kid ever find a job? Only if he stays away from salad bars.

Or stumbles across a classified as follows:

"WANTED: One paranoid, anal-retentive individual, incapable of anticipating the unexpected, with limited numerical skills and prone to lapses in concentration.

Bad breath a plus."

Declaring 18th Century Independence With 21st Century tools

IN A LATER CHAPTER I WILL DISCUSS, IN LENGTHY AND MORE BORING detail, the business community's increasing reliance on PowerPoint. Yes, corporate America truly loves its high tech tools—tools that have taken simple tasks that could be completed in an hour and turned them into affairs lasting weeks, months, or until the project manager gets fired, at which time the process starts anew. While today's business workers wonder how in the world anybody was able to achieve results without the aid of conference calls, email, text messages, and the nitpicking and backstabbing that accompanies the use of said tools, fact is, the reverse is true. Some of history's greatest moments may have turned out alarmingly different were companies like Apple, Verizon, and Microsoft allowed to get involved. Case in point? The writing of the Declaration of Independence. Drafted over a 16-day period[13] and written entirely in fountain pen, the document can be seen by more than one million visitors yearly at the

---

13   The time it takes to conduct the average conference call today

---

National Archives in Washington, DC. The only reason the document remains is because it was not typed on a PC, hence nobody was able to inadvertently click, "yes," when an onscreen pop up appeared asking, "Are you SURE you want to delete this."

Of course I'm not suggesting this country would still toil under British rule if our forefathers tried to proclaim independence with today's business tools. Composing the Declaration itself was only part of our nation's launch; a ragtag band of soldiers still had to defeat a disciplined army of British fighters with muskets capable of firing a single shot every one minute and 38 seconds[14]. But drafting the document may have played out in an entirely different manner were they able to stock up on time-saving tools from the local Best Buy. To wit:

THOMAS JEFFERSON: Okay, let this meeting of the Founding Fathers come to order. Is everybody present and accounted for?

BEN FRANKLIN: Just about. Hancock will be calling in from Massachusetts. I've got the conference line all set up. Strange, I thought he'd be on by now.

JEFFERSON: Ping him.

FRANKLIN: Great idea. Wait, there he is.

JOHN HANCOCK: Can everybody hear me?

JEFFERSON: Loud and clear. Let's get started. For the guys in this room, do we want to order some food first?

JOHN ADAMS: Couldn't we have done that off line?

FRANKLIN: Everybody just text me your orders. I'll email the Silversmith Saloon.

JEFFERSON: Okay, we have a lot of writing to do and, wait, Hancock is that your dog barking?

HANCOCK: Sorry, let me move to another room. Can everybody hear me now?

---

14   The amount of time it took some dude wearing a Revolutionary War uniform to do it on YouTube

JEFFERSON: You're good. Now, did everybody get the first draft? I called it "Independence v1."

BENJAMIN HARRISON: Mine was all garbled.

JEFFERSON: You didn't upgrade to the latest version of Word, did you?

HARRISON: Why can't we just use Google Docs? Or Dropbox?

HANCOCK: Because I don't want papers with my signature floating around in the cloud. You know how prevalent identity theft is in the colonies.

JEFFERSON: Tell me about it. Some guy swiped my identity last week and bought this huge house in Monticello posing as me! What a mess.

ADAMS: Ben, what's with the video camera?

FRANKLIN: I'm recording this for YouTube. This thing is going to go viral, baby.

ADAMS: You really think people are going to watch a bunch of guys in powdered wigs sitting around a table?

HARRISON: I'd rather watch cat videos myself. By the way, did everybody see the one where the cat gets caught in the laundry hamper and ends up wearing a sweater? It was adorable. Check it out.

JEFFERSON: Gentlemen we have now been here 15 minutes and accomplished nothing. Let's go over the opening sentence, "When in the Course of human events it becomes necessary for one people to dissolve the political bands which have connected them with another and to assume among the powers of the earth, the separate and equal station to which the Laws of Nature and of Nature's God entitle them, a decent respect to the opinions of mankind requires that they should declare the causes which impel them to the separation." Thoughts?

(BEEPING SOUND HEARD FROM SPEAKER)

HANCOCK: ink...at's...irdy

JEFFERSON: John, you're breaking up. Where are you?

HANCOCK: Can you hear me now? How about now? Now?

JEFFERSON: Much better. Now, what were you saying?

DOG: Woof. Howl. Bark.

HANCOCK: Sorry. My dog followed me into the other room. I said, "I think that's too wordy." And not bold enough. Has anybody used the online thesaurus? Maybe we could punch it up, especially that part about "separate and equal station."

FRANKLIN: Checking the thesaurus now. How about "detached and identical rank?" Sound any better?

HARRISON: It wouldn't be my first choice, but whatever anybody else wants is fine with me.

JEFFERSON: Okay, we'll make that change. Next?

HANCOCK: I'm not entirely on board with it, not that anybody cares what my opinion is. After all, it's only my signature on it.

JEFFERSON: John, do you like it or not?

HANCOCK: No, really. It's fine. I've got another conference call in 15 minutes so let's move on.

FRANKLIN: Tom, what font were you planning on using?

JEFFERSON: Well, that's open to debate too. I think Goudy Stout makes a real statement.

HANCOCK: You're joking, right? Rockwell is the only way to go.

FRANKLIN: Gentlemen, please. Any font will do but, because we are declaring independence from England, I suggest we don't use Old English Text MT. Ditto for Georgia. Do not introduce anything named "George" into this document.

HARRISON: Are we going to include humor in this declaration? That part about, "He has erected a multitude of New Offices, and sent hither swarms of Officers to harass our people and eat out their substance," is kind of funny. Maybe it's because we say "erected." That makes me giggle. So how about Comic Sans MS?

JEFFERSON: Are you sure we want to say "eat out?"

JOHN PENN: ♋▤♏●♓□□❖🖼

JEFFERSON: John, how many times have we told you, we can't understand you when you talk in "Wing Dings?"

FRANKLIN: Sorry. Can't we just use Times New Roman and move on?

JEFFERSON: Roman. So medieval. But, okay.

HANCOCK: Hey guys, I have to jump off the line for just a minute. I'll catch up. Work on slide two in my absence.

FRANKLIN: Are the slides going to advance automatically or will George have to use a mouse?

PENN: What if his mouse isn't working?

ADAMS: But if they advance automatically, he may miss something.

JEFFERSON: We could overnight him a mouse. Does Fed Ex deliver to England?

ADAMS: I'm sure his IT director can walk him through it if he has trouble. So we're cool on the introduction. By the way, I was thinking that George's tyrannical reign could best be displayed with an org chart.

FRANKLIN: So you don't like the line, "we hold these truths to be self-evident?"

ADAMS: That's not what I said. But, a picture is worth a thousand words. So if we do an old org chart with him at the top and then show, in slide 3, a new org chart with say, George Washington in his place, now we're really driving the point home.

FRANKLIN: Washington? At the top? He's not even part of this meeting. And now you're nominating him for President? Was I out of the room when that decision occurred?

JEFFERSON: Nothing's etched in stone, Ben. We were kicking it around at the pub last night over pints of Sam Adams.

SAM ADAMS: I have a beer named after me? Who knew? By the way, wasn't somebody supposed to bring bagels today?

HANCOCK: Okay, I'm back. Can someone catch me up?

FRANKLIN: Apparently George Washington is going to be our first president, not that everybody got a say in that. So much for democracy.

ADAMS: Can we stay on task please? Are we in favor of the org chart replacing the phrase "we hold these truths to be self-evident?"

JEFFERSON: I'm cool with it. What about listing our grievances? So far we have 27.

HANCOCK: Right. And we need bullet points for all of them.

JOHN ADAMS: But don't list more than five per screen. That muddies it up. Wait, did somebody else just join?

JAMES MADISON: (ON SPEAKER PHONE) Sorry I'm late. Did I miss anything?

FRANKLIN: Not unless you had your heart set on being the first president. Washington just took that title. Even though he's not here.

MADISON: Where is he anyway?

JEFFERSON: Scoping out some place called Valley Forge, I think. He thinks it might be a good winter getaway for the troops.

MADISON: Where in King George's name is Valley Forge?

JEFFERSON: No idea. I plugged it into Google Maps and nothing came back!

HANCOCK: Gentlemen, please! Do we agree that slides 4-7 should be a bulleted list of grievances?

FRANKLIN: Wait a minute. Have we even discussed slide background? What color are we planning on using?

HANCOCK: Red. It symbolizes blood.

JEFFERSON: I think blue would be better. It reminds me of open skies and freedom. That's what this is all about.

SAM ADAMS: Can't we just go with basic white?

HANCOCK: I can see we're getting nowhere with this. Let's just compromise. How about red, white and blue?

ALL: Aye.

MADISON: Hey guys, my battery is about to die. How should we end this?

HANCOCK: Well, we've got the line, "that these United Colonies are, and of Right ought to be, FREE AND INDEPENDENT STATES; that they are absolved from all Allegiance to the British Crown." That's good, but we can do so much more.

ADAMS: Why don't we embed a link to our web site in the final slide? In bold letters?

HANCOCK: Great idea. The website looks fantastic, by the way. Our web designer did some really cool stuff with Java Script.

SAM ADAMS: What's the web address again? USA.gov, right?

MADISON: That's what we hoped it would be. But some online porn company snatched it up. I was on that site last night and saw colonial women doing things that should definitely be illegal once we start writing laws. So we had to go with USofA.gov.

JEFFERSON: Oh my God! My laptop just crashed.

HANCOCK: You saved your work, right?

JEFFERSON: Aaaaaaaaaah!

ALL: Aaaaaaaaaaah!

IV

Anatomy of a Corporate Website

ONE DAY, IN 1983, MY FATHER CAME HOME MIDAFTERNOON, immediately retreated to our basement, and launched a business.

This was before suburban homeowners looked at basements as potential entertainment centers that could literally double a home's square footage just by installing carpeting, Pop-a-Shot games, and bars featuring taps that gush foul tasting home-brewed beer proudly created by a Dad in the midst of a major mid-life crisis. I've even seen basements in my neighborhood that contain, among other toys, DJ booths, disco balls, wine cellars, movie theatres, golf simulators, and video gaming systems so realistic, the U.S. Department of Defense comes by once a month to check out the latest shoot 'em up titles. A neighbor down the street actually makes a *living* taking underground rooms comprised of nothing more than exposed pipes and sump pumps and turning them into something that a family of six could easily live in, providing they have no interest in looking outside, due to the lack of windows.

Growing up, our basement contained a rickety ping pong game, a long wooden table—half of which was covered with Mom's sewing machine and accessories—and that's about it. Dad simply took the unused half of the table, placed a single-line phone on top, snaked a lengthy cord along the wall so it reached the phone jack at the basement's other end, stole the adding machine from the kitchen, placed his prize silver Cross pen and pencil set on top of a desk blotter he purchased at the local Walgreens, and announced that his boss was an incorrigible asshole. From this moment on, Dad continued, he would be running his own company, in direct competition with aforementioned asshole.

That company continued until Dad retired in 1998. A table, a pen, and a Rolodex were his tools. Many times he hinted that I should go into the business with him but, as I mentioned in the initial chapter, I respectfully—and sometimes not so respectfully—declined. Doing so before the dawn of technology spared me from having to collaborate with him on building what has become the centerpiece of a business today: The company website.

I can actually visualize the arguments in my head:

Dad, we need a social networking presence!

We've already got one. I'm very social. You can't be a damn salesman for 40 years and not be social.

Dad, we need a B2B and a B2C channel.

What we need is for you to get your lazy ass on the phone and start cold calling.

Dad, we need live chat.

What do you think you and I are doing right now? We're chatting and we're both alive although, judging from the business you've brought in during the past quarter, I'm starting to question that. My last salesman had better results than you and he died seven years ago!

Yes, now one can't even *think* of opening a business without first constructing a web site. The site can be as simple as one page that says basically, "if you've found this page, let us know how you did it," to sites built by international corporations that first ask, in English, what language you speak? Anybody who doesn't speak or read English has no choice to but to hit the "back" button and return to surfing porn, which is understandable in any language.

The web is truly littered with sites for companies, products, and services; never mind that many of those three no longer exist. The Internet is like that hall closet in your house. Occasionally you need to open the door, clean out all the crap that is no longer of use to anybody, and close it again. Unfortunately, that's not the case in cyberspace, which is why it is still possible to run across websites that haven't been updated since the Internet's infancy.

If you want to see the evolution of a website, look no further than the Internet Archive Wayback Machine.[15] The machine is actually a "service," that allows visitors to index archived versions of websites, dating all the way back to 1996[16]. In other words, if you've surfed every site on the Internet and are still bored, you can begin surfing sites from the past. If that's too much trouble, turn off your PC, and watch the *Nick at Nite* channel, featuring television shows from the 1970s. Once you've done that, there is nothing more to do in life.

Included in the Wayback machine are earlier web versions of enduring companies like Microsoft. But what fun is that? It's far more entertaining to surf sites touting some of history's most spectacular dotcom busts. Anyone remember Flooz.com? The company hoped it's online currency, or "Flooz," would replace credit cards. Instead of paying with plastic, one paid with varying amounts of Flooz, taken from one's online Flooz account. This new money system lead to guys in bars turning to their buddies and saying, "Yo Steve, can you spot me 20? I'm a little short of Flooz 'til next Friday."

Launched in 1998, Flooz.com was dead and buried by 2001, in spite of the fact that it had raised $35 million in cash and Flooz and signed up some humungous companies as customers. While the Flooz.com website

---

15   www.archive.org

16   the year Al Gore invented the Internet

has been eliminated from the web[17], its presence remains on the Wayback Machine, which notes that the Flooz site grew from four simple pages in 1999 to 166 pages by the time it ran out of Flooz.

There are two types of corporate websites. The first are those like Flooz. com, where the website basically IS the business, meaning that if not for the web, the company would not exist. I've always thought YouTube fell into that category. That was, until I met Salar Kamangar, at the time the CEO of YouTube and living proof that YouTube has actual employees. Kamangar was among the guests at a corporate skiing retreat in Park City, Utah. I found it amazing Kamangar had time to go skiing considering his title. Any person who must approve millions of hours of inane videos ranging from a baby's first steps to bored teenagers placing random household objects in microwaves surely must have a full day planner. I had hoped to corner Kamangar with my suggestion on how to thin out the number of YouTube videos [18] —begin by eliminating anything featuring a pet, a cleansing process that should cut the number at least by half—but the man was heading out the door holding ski poles.

The second are those with actual brick and mortar presences, meaning every day employees enter a building made of bricks and mortar and sit there miserably for eight hours. The website was created only so prospective customers never have to see this environment.

The Wayback Machine confirms that most websites started off as a few simple pages, containing only the most pertinent information and void of video testimonials from satisfied customers who stare at a camera and say, "We couldn't do what we do without the help of FlixTex. Whatever it is we do, FlixTex helps us do it better." Today, the average corporate website now contains approximately 4,327,859 of the most awesome, most original, most eye-popping, most "click-here-and-all-your-personal-contact-information-will-be-secretly-uploaded-to-our-servers" pages in all of cyberspace. Furthermore, the company is convinced that visitors are

---

17   Most likely by Whoopi Goldberg, the official Flooz spokesperson

18   One hundred new hours of video are uploaded every minute

---

actually looking at every single whitepaper, brochure, slide presentation, graphic, and video clip before ultimately finding the answer they had originally been seeking: "Does Joe from accounting still work here?"

That's the problem with the Internet: Without discipline, there is no end in sight. How often have you become so engrossed in the web that you actually forgot how you ended up on a particular page?

Let's see, I think I sat down about five hours ago to pay bills online. Then I navigated over to my stock portfolio and saw that my IRA had dropped 15 percent. That's when I realized that my kids' college tuition might be in jeopardy so I Googled, "potential athletic scholarships." That made me realize that the Cubs game was on so I clicked on ESPN to check the score and then I got into a chat room with other Cubs fans, one of whom sent me a YouTube clip titled, "Great Moments in Cubs History."[19] So I was watching that and there was a real cool music soundtrack playing in the background and I wanted to know what song it was so I Googled the lyrics and...that's why I'm now reading all about Kid Rock on Wikipedia!

In reality, a good corporate website needs only a few features to serve its purpose, which is to make us all wonder why the hell we can't return to the basement:

1) What We Do

Contrary to popular belief, the "What We Do" link[20] was not created for the potential customer. It exists solely for company employees who are sitting in their cubicles at 3:20 p.m., surrounded by brick and mortar, and suddenly can't remember their purpose for existing. With glazed looks in their eyes and slight drool streams running down their chins, they suddenly start mumbling semi-incoherent rants like, "Why am I here?", "Where is my car parked?," and "Why do I have to stay here until five o'clock?", before somebody reminds them to click "What We Do" and read the first few sentences. That typically does the trick.

---

19   It's a very short video, trust me!

20   Also known as "About Us," or "Our Company"

What amazes me is that, often after clicking "What We Do," and reading the contents, most company employees act surprised. Their expressions say, "Ahhhhh, now it makes sense," even though most "What We Do" descriptions make absolutely no sense because whoever wrote it graduated from the school of "why use 10 words when 100 words will do?" For example, go to the Pfizer website,[21] click "About Pfizer" and you will learn that the company has "a leading portfolio of products and medicines that support wellness and prevention, as well as treatment and cures for diseases across a broad range of therapeutic areas." That's corporate speak for "We help 80-year-old men get hard."

The onslaught of technology brought with it a cavalcade[22] of useless corporate phrases that now accompany every description of a company's purpose and are designed to do nothing more than make potential customers spend money simply because whomever wrote that phrase must be REALLY, REALLY smart. That's why "What We Do" descriptions typically sound like this: "We competently engineer e-business outsourcing by seamlessly scaling client-based mindshare while efficiently disseminating functional services, resulting in holistically driven sticky best practices."[23]

Often companies contradict themselves when trying to explain exactly what it is they do. Witness Phillip Morris, the world's largest manufacturer of tobacco products or fatal diseases, depending on whom you ask. Phillip Morris has always had to tap dance around the issue of manufacturing a product that comes with warning labels; it appears they have only confused themselves in the process as evidenced by their "What We Do" website verbiage: "We want adult cigarette smokers of our brands to purchase our brands consistently. Likewise, we want adult cigarette smokers of competitor brands to switch to our brands. While we want to grow our market share within the cigarette industry, we do not want adults to start smoking nor do we want kids to start smoking."

---

21   www.boners.biz

22   "Cavalcade?" Did I really just type "cavalcade?"

23   In other words, "We make awesome lattes!"

In other words, our stock price will remain strong and, by working here, you will be able to afford a summer home in Michigan because somehow, some way we'll make sure kids start smoking.

2) History

It's also important to let customers know how many years it took to go from a fiscally sound organization, to one teetering on the edge of bankruptcy. That's why the "history" link is so important. As a consumer I'm not *always* concerned with a company's timeline—I've never gone into Wal-Mart, said, "Where is the toilet paper?", and followed it up with, "And exactly how long have you been selling it?—but it's of vital importance to other companies. You wouldn't fly on an airline that sprang up in 2011, would you?

The history page should contain one sentence: "We were founded in INSERT YEAR HERE and unlike Flooz.com, we are still around." Unfortunately, like the "What We Do" link, some companies have found it necessary to give the most detailed timeline available, convinced that customers will flock to a company that had a presence in another century. I recently performed a show for Ziegler, "a specialty investment bank with unique expertise in complex credit structures and advisory services." (HUH?) When I clicked the "history" tab, I learned that "in 1902, BC 'Ben' Ziegler started an insurance business in West Bend, Wisconsin and made loans to farmers." However, at first reading, I failed to note the inclusion of a comma in that previous sentence and assumed the company had been around since 1902 BC. "How cool," I thought, "to have a guy selling insurance to the Mycenaeans shortly after they gained control of Greece!"

3) Products and Solutions

Typically these words are used interchangeably because really, no company wants to give the impression that it's possible to come up with a solution without buying a product. Of course this runs counter to, say, parenting, where the best solutions usually take place after *removing* a product e.g. "if your grades don't improve, we are going to take away your cell phone."

The products/solutions section is where it becomes possible to immerse yourself in the site for so long that you forget your kids' birthdays have come and gone and you are still wearing the same clothes that you wore six months ago when you sat down at the PC. Take, for example, IBM. Before finding a solution, the user must first figure out what part of IBM is going to offer assistance. Can IBM help you in the field of aerospace and defense, automotive, banking, chemicals and petroleum, construction, consumer products, education, electronics, financial markets, forest and paper, government, healthcare, insurance, life sciences, media and entertainment, metals and mining, retail, telecommunications or travel, and transportation? Or did you just visit the site to find out how you can become as smart as Watson?[24]

For the heck of it, I chose banking. From there I was asked whether I needed a solution for my front office or my back office. Was I interested in integrated risk management or banking solutions for a smarter planet? Did I want to watch video of some IBM employees with very long, hard to pronounce names that could explain what IBM was doing when it came to providing banking solutions? Did I want to read IBM banking case studies? Or view the IBM Banking Industry framework? Maybe I wanted to join the SmarterFinancial Services LinkedIn group or follow @ IBMBanking on Twitter.

Actually, I was interested in purchasing one of those little laptop thingies.

Of course, anybody who has ever ordered a computer online knows that it involves answering more questions than your average three year old poses in an afternoon, which is why many companies, as part of their websites, employ a useful feature called…

---

24   In February 2011, an IBM computer named Watson soundly defeated two human *Jeopardy* champs, proving that computers know more than we do about 18th century Latin poets.

---

4. Chat Now

Usually this link is accessed by clicking on the image of a perky looking, 20-something individual wearing a headset who, judging by his or her expression, CAN'T WAIT to speak with you about your insurance, medical, or computer needs.

In reality, this person is 47 and sitting in a cubicle bank that begins in New Delhi, India and stops somewhere around Vietnam. But, that's not important. What IS important is that this person is willing to chat however you want to chat. Want a phone call? Just type in your number, wait about five seconds, and perky chat representative #1 will be on your caller ID. Prefer to chat online? Just click the icon and yet another window will open on your screen, notifying you that you are the 357th person in cue and to please be patient even though you are most likely standing on a 35th-story ledge because your computer is malfunctioning. Want to be notified by mail? Sorry, not gonna happen. That's why the company launched a website—so it wouldn't have to communicate via the U.S. Postal Service.

Chatting with someone who actually knows what he or she is doing is a concept that has been around long before it was possible to reveal all your personal information while letting a chat room tech "take over" your PC. In 1981, six female home economists decided they would rather do ANYTHING other than spend Thanksgiving Day with their families, leading to formation of the Butterball Turkey Talk Line. Today the number has grown by leaps and bounds and even includes male turkey experts, proving that men are just as adept as women when it comes to picking up a phone and calmly explaining to a panicked first time turkey cooker that Domino's Pizza is open on Thanksgiving Day.

I actually applied to be one of those "turkey technicians" even though my turkey preparation skills are maddeningly inconsistent. Dry and overcooked one year, shockingly underdone the next. But, by the fifth year of hosting relatives for the annual food and football blowout, I had the technique down, meaning I no longer let Aunt Trudy, (not her real name since she's still alive), enter the kitchen, open the oven and offer "tips" such as, "it looks a tad pink to me," "next year, tie the legs tighter," and "you're out of vodka." Mind you, all of these conversations occurred while I was sharpening a monstrous carving knife. Such is the beauty of Thanksgiving.

I didn't really want to be a Turkey Talk Line tech; I just wanted to answer one phone call and put some poor, hapless first time chef through the rigors that accompany asking complete strangers for help. I even submitted some sample dialogue to Butterball as part of my audition:

"Butterball Hot Line. This is Greg. May I help you?"

"Hi, this is Emily from Seattle...

"Is it raining right now in Seattle?"

"Yes, but that's not why I'm calling. My turkey..."

"So it's raining and you screwed up your turkey? Wow, I thought I was depressed."

"I didn't screw it up. At least I don't think I did. But it's been roasting for eight hours and it still doesn't look done."

"Eight hours? Hmm, let me check the manual. (LOUD RUSTLING OF PAGES) Oh my God, Emily, GET OUT OF THE HOUSE NOW! AND GET YOUR AFFAIRS IN ORDER!!"

"Excuse me?"

"Just kidding. That makes everybody laugh around here. Marge in the next cubicle almost peed her pants. Hey, can you check the football score for me? Butterball doesn't have TVs in this room."

"Um, it's 17-14 Cowboys."

"Excellent. Romo's on my Fantasy team."

"Who cares? I need help. My relatives are starving and I don't know what to do."

"That's why you have side dishes Emily. Want me to transfer you to the green bean/crunchy onion hotline? How about the mashed potatoes hotline? Are you making gravy? If so, hold times are a bit longer."

"No, no, no! Look, the thermometer says 165. Is that sufficient?"

"Depends. Are we talking Fahrenheit or Celsius?"

"Fahrenheit! Why would I use a Celsius thermometer?"

"Maybe you have European relatives. The turkey's done Emily. Take it out."

"Okay, but now I need help carving. What kind of knife should I use?"

"Knife? Who uses knives? A simple karate chop should do. I once saw a guy on *America's Got Talent* break three bricks with his head."

"Karate chop the turkey? You can't be serious."

"Of course I'm serious Emily. I'm a trained professional."

"All right. Hold on." (LOUD THUMP FOLLOWED BY SHRIEK OF PAIN) "That didn't work."

"You must have hit the stuffing."

"Can I speak to your supervisor?"

"Hold on. (PAUSE) Aunt Trudy, pick up on line two."

I've tried chatting via phone and instant messaging and prefer the latter because it allows me to multi-task while I'm waiting in cue. Even when a customer service rep gets online and I begin typing my question or problem, I'm still free to update my Facebook page, tweet about how long I've been holding, or scream at my kids should they choose to enter the room while I am trying to communicate with unseen "help." Trust me, phone support reps get confused when you are talking with them about a particular issue and then suddenly scream, "CLEAN YOUR ROOM," mid-sentence.

Depending on how sophisticated a company's "Chat Now" function is, wait time can be minimal. Sometimes too minimal. I once clicked "Chat Now," expecting to be placed into a holding cue, which would give me time to compose my message succinctly. Instead, mere seconds after clicking, the support rep responded with, "Good afternoon! How may I help you today?" Flustered, I could only type the first thought that came in to my head:

"What are you wearing?"

Needless to say, Jeffrey from tech support was not amused.

Once a company establishes a live help presence, it must properly train its employees. This consists of telling the employees to repeat every single word the customer says, as if the two were talking in a wind tunnel or a disco. Example:

HELP DESK: Hello. My name is Sanreet. Thank you for contacting Dell Computer Support. How may I be of service today?

CUSTOMER: I want to inquire about updating the software on my Dell Inspiron 580 PC.

HELP DESK: Let me make sure I am understanding you correctly. You have a Dell Inspiron 580 PC?

CUSTOMER: Correct.

HELP DESK: And you wish to update the software on it?

CUSTOMER: Yes.

HELP DESK: The software that runs your Inspiron?

CUSTOMER: Yes, what else would it be running?

HELP DESK: There are many types of computers available today.

CUSTOMER: I understand that.

HELP DESK: And which type of computer do you own?

CUSTOMER: The Inspiron 580.

HELP DESK: Have you recently performed a software upgrade?

CUSTOMER: Uh no. Isn't that why we are chatting?

HELP DESK: I have no idea. You initiated this chat.

CUSTOMER: Right…to upgrade the software.

HELP DESK: On your Inspiron 580?

CUSTOMER: Yes

HELP DESK: You can find upgrade information on our website simply by clicking http://www.upgradesoftware.com/$%^&*(%$#^/_@#$!!! xv45?{}|?WTF?

CUSTOMER: I will click on that link now. Please don't leave me. I'm begging you.

HELP DESK: I will stay with you even though I am chatting with 73 other customers and sending them helpful web links similar to yours.

CUSTOMER: I just tried that link and it only pertains to the Inspiron 580x.

HELP DESK: Would you like to purchase a 580x? Right now we are offering free shipping.

CUSTOMER: No, I just purchased the 580. Why would I need the 580x?

HELP DESK: Because we have upgraded the software.

CUSTOMER: Can you upgrade the software for me?

HELP DESK: I'm sorry but I cannot.

CUSTOMER: Why not?

HELP DESK: For more assistance, please click the "What We Do" link. Thank you for contacting us.

V

A History of Billionaires and Why They Keep Getting Richer

To: *Mr. Greg Schwein*

Subject: *Your inheritance awaits!*

Dear Mr. Schwump:

I am emailing you on behalf of my deceased Nigerian client, Prince Kufour Otumfuo the elder son of the late King Otumfuo Opoku and half-brother to George Clooney. As I'm sure you read in Nigerian Weekly World News, the prince was recently murdered by either UFOs or Al Qaeda. You have been identified as a family member and are therefore eligible to receive a share of the Prince's $87.3 billion fortune. Currently the money is being held in "Nigerian Escrow," meaning it's buried under a desert cactus. To claim your share, please email me your social security number, copy of your driver's license, Google Earth-captured photos of your home, and any other personal information you feel would be helpful. What's left of the Otumfuo family thanks you. P.S. you also may have won an extra one million dollars in the Publisher's Clearinghouse sweepstakes!

Growing up in suburban Chicago, my friends and I liked to toss the word "billion" around in casual conversation. It was used in one of three contexts:

» We were proud of our family dynamics ("My Dad is a billion times smarter than your Dad.")

» We were stressed ("I have a billion hours of homework this weekend.")

» We were stoned ("Dude, the chemicals in that Twinkie could be, like, 4 billion years old.")

Today it is perfectly normal to speak of something in the billions without the aid of pharmaceuticals or the need to sing your family's praises. This is especially true when the subject is individual wealth—or the nation's national debt in the 1700s. Today that figure is more than 17 trillion dollars, equal to Oprah Winfrey's net worth had she not spent most of the early 21st century giving away cars to studio audience members.[25]

Billionaires, while not stomping around in packs al a *The Walking Dead* characters, have become prevalent enough to warrant an annual list compiled by *Forbes* Magazine, a business publication that does nothing except create lists that will never include my name or yours. A 2014 list of the world's billionaires contained over 1,000 names of individuals who have amassed 99.9999 percent of the world's wealth, despite not having any deceased Nigerian relatives. The remaining .0001 percent is currently being counted in a Las Vegas casino, spent by tourists who think the only way to become a billionaire is to repeatedly hit the Megabucks jackpot.

Forbes' entrants ranged from the self-made billionaire, (casino magnate Sheldon Adelson was the son of a taxi driver and a knitting shop owner), to the family inheritance billionaire, (Charlene de Carvalho-Heineken sensed she might be worth something after entering a convenience store

---

25 In 2004 all 276 audience members received Pontiac G-6 midsize sports sedans, which they promptly sold on eBay

for a 12-pack in college and spying her last name on green bottles that had been placed just down the aisle from the beef jerky. Reluctantly, her family told her).

I have met and conversed with exactly two billionaires in my life. Well, two that I know of. I may have inadvertently met others, but I can't think of a single scenario where I would have encountered one by chance. Most billionaires don't fly economy class, coach Little League, attend Brownie meetings, or eat long lunches at Panera Bread simply to take advantage of the free Wi-Fi. Instead, I met both at business conferences, where billionaires are often invited to speak on whatever they darn well please as long as the speech contains at least one investment tip. Many billionaires add to their wealth by casually mentioning a "must own" stock midway through a speech. Every audience member immediately becomes Pavlov's dog, whipping out cell phones in unison and purchasing 100 shares via online brokerage sites. They don't realize the billionaire purchased the stock an hour earlier at a much lower price.

The first billionaire I encountered was former Microsoft CEO Steve Ballmer. It was backstage at, naturally, a large business conference and Ballmer was pacing the corridor as if he were about to attempt a Super Bowl-game-winning field goal. His facial expressions and tics were proof that even billionaires can't purchase calm. Ballmer was obviously rehearsing his remarks so I elected not to bother him other than to say, "Why would I switch to Microsoft Outlook Express when I'm already using Outlook?" He appeared stumped.

The second billionaire whose air I temporarily breathed was T. Boone Pickens, the flamboyant oilman and guest speaker at a convention of automotive software employees in Southern California. True to his oilman persona, Pickens showed up for his outdoor speech wearing a sharply tailored brown suit, accessorized with cowboy boots, a 10-gallon hat and a gargantuan silver belt buckle that temporarily blinded all audience members sitting in the first three rows. Pickens' speech consisted of pining for the policies of Ronald Reagan and predicting the upcoming fortunes of Oklahoma State football, a team that has benefitted from Pickens' largesse. Pickens has dunked so much money into the team's coffers that his name not only adorns the stadium, but is also required to be mentioned in every offensive huddle.

Guys, it's third and long. Let's run the 'Pickens slant.' Snap on 'Boone.' Ready, Break!

In spite of his "aw shucks," Southern drawl and demeanor, Pickens struck me as a guy who would vow revenge if you did something as innocuous as beat him in a game of horseshoes. Maybe it was the hat. Attire someone in a pair of blue jeans, a bolo tie, and a 10-gallon hat and it screams, "Redneck who rides horses." But, put that same guy in a tailored suit, topped off with the same hat, and suddenly it shouts, "Successful businessman who can hogtie you if absolutely necessary."

The one thing Pickens and Ballmer have in common is that they are business people, proving that, only in the world of business is it possible to amass wealth in the billions. Even today's professional athletes don't, as of yet, sign billion dollar contracts. Basketball legend Michael Jordan is the only billionaire athlete, a fact revealed by *Forbes* in its, (surprise!), "World's Highest Paid Athletes" list but the bulk of his wealth comes from investments, commercial endorsements, and his ownership stake in the Charlotte Hornets. In short, business.

Another "down home" billionaire is Warren Buffet, best known as being the only billionaire who has failed to realize Nebraska is a horrible place to live if you have money. Dubbed the "Oracle of Omaha" for his ability to forecast, with uncanny accuracy, the long term success of a company as well as how many tornadoes will strike Nebraska in a calendar year, Buffet made his fortune as the head of Berkshire Hathaway, an investment company that encourages ordinary citizens to invest in some of the most boring companies in existence. Yes, I'm talking about you Precision Castparts, manufacturer of forged components and airfoil castings!

Buffet is also one of the world's most accessible billionaires, providing your bank account also contains nine digits. Each year eBay auctions off, "Lunch with Warren Buffet," with all proceeds going to GLIDE, a San Francisco-based charity. The winning bidder and seven friends get the opportunity to dine with Buffet at Smith & Wollensky in New York City. In 2015, Chinese gaming magnate Zhu He paid $2.35 million for a chance to eat a T-bone steak and glean investment advice. Reportedly, the first thing Buffet told Mr. He was that paying $2.35 million for lunch is a stupid investment.

When I Googled, "Who was the world's first billionaire?" I was surprised at the result. I would have thought it was God since church collection plates worldwide are loaded weekly with cash and checks for His benefit. Instead, to my surprise, the answer was...

John D. Rockefeller

Born in 1839, Rockefeller proved that it is possible to amass a billion dollar fortune without creating a dating app. The son of a con artist/elixir salesman, (QUICK PARENTING LESSON: Lie, cheat and swindle if you want your kids to be successful!), Rockefeller went to work as an accountant and discovered a passion for numbers, something I assume most accountants must eventually do if they plan to continue their craft. Somehow the ability to add, subtract, and multiply lead to Rockefeller forming Standard Oil, a fact I mention to my children whenever possible. ("How can you expect to be a billionaire when you only scored 68 out of 70 on your fractions test?") Rockefeller's checkered history included monopolistic business practices that put him squarely at odds with other tycoons racing to become known as "the world's second billionaire." Eventually Rockefeller retired to upstate New York where he took up golf and learned, on the first day, that all the money in the world will never make one a better short iron player. Rockefeller's legacy included an $80 million gift to the University of Chicago, formation of the Rockefeller

Institute for Medical Research (known today as Rockefeller University) and a last name synonymous with wealth and prestige. In 1974, President Gerald Ford tapped Nelson Rockefeller to be his vice president in spite of the latter's limited political experience. Ford made the choice only because he thought Rockefeller could wipe out the national debt by writing a single check from his "rainy day" account.

John D. Rockefeller's billions put him far ahead of other business tycoons in the 18th and 19th centuries, even though their net worth's were no slouch. Henry Morrison Flagler, a Rockefeller partner in the formation of Standard Oil, made his billions in the railway sector, eventually opening up the east coast of Florida to transportation which is a nice way of saying Flagler founded "Spring Break in Fort Lauderdale." He also founded the town of Palm Beach, a vacation enclave ironically loaded with residents who wouldn't set foot on a train unless all avenues of private jet transportation had been exhausted. Palm Beach is home to assorted millionaires, billionaires, Kennedys, and Donald Trump, who continues reminding society that he is richer than anybody because he created a reality show.

Secretly though, Trump knows he will never reach the echelon of the world's most well-known billionaires, all of whom have achieved their wealth by creating products the world cannot do without, and working together to ensure they all simultaneously benefit from each other's success. First and foremost is the world richest individual, none other than...

Bill Gates

When Gates unleashed Microsoft software on the public he wisely inserted a paragraph into the "Terms of Use/Click 'Yes' if you Accept/ Sure We'll Click 'Yes' Because We Don't Have Time to Read This Incomprehensible Lawyer-Created Drivel."

Using a magnifying glass or microscope, read Paragraph 394, Section 115, subsection 27.b, which SPECIFICALLY states:

I, Bill Gates, will collect $100,000 each time you open this Microsoft program.

This sentence is why Microsoft pushes the idea of multitasking—running multiple programs simultaneously. If a user on a conference call is staring at a Word document, along with an Excel spread sheet and a PowerPoint presentation, Gates' monetary haul increases threefold.

Once Gates realized that nobody, not even Michael Jordan, would match his wealth, he set about apologizing for the monster he created. In a 2013 speech at Harvard, Gates' almost alma mater, he declared the Control+Alt+Delete function used to reboot PCs was a mistake. Okay, Gates blamed the keyboard move—which requires using two hands unless you're a computer-savvy octopus —on an IBM engineer but, hey, it was still a startling admission from a guy who invented three hour hold times for users forced to call technical support after their computers froze while playing Microsoft Solitaire during conference calls.

The whole world waited for Gates to continue in confession mode. Microsoft users didn't demand refunds or lobby the Justice Department to launch an investigation; instead they hoped Gates would issue the following statement:

Thank you, world, for hearing my confession. For those of you trying to hear it via an online connection, that's confession number one: Internet Explorer sucks.

Confession number two: I knew all along about a little hiccup in Microsoft Word. But, I didn't know it would cause graduate students to lose their entire thesis papers 45 minutes before they were due. For those of you who suffered permanent disfigurement when you drove your fist through a computer monitor, I am truly sorry.

I apologize for the 'blue screen of death' that contained unintelligible messages like 'Fatal Error X01XXXXX000003.' Had I known some users would actually die from burst blood vessels upon seeing that screen, I would have replaced it with something more soothing: a purring kitten perhaps.

I apologize for the paper clip that mockingly questioned your decision to exit a program, asking, 'Are you sure?' We thought it was a safety feature; in reality, I should have known that nobody likes to feel belittled by an office supply product.

I apologize for Windows 98. When we released it, most people, myself included, were still trying to master the intricacies of Windows 95. Our next version should have been called 'Windows 2011—Install It If You Dare.'

I apologize that Microsoft Publisher gave you the ability to bypass a professional printer and create your own wedding invitations. Your frugality caused many people to skip your wedding by assuming, correctly, that your homemade invitations meant you were also employing a cash bar at the reception.

I apologize for Microsoft Excel. Where do I even begin?

I apologize for Xbox. To all kids and male adults who spend hours playing Halo and all of its reincarnations, I have a message: Put the joystick down and go outside. A little sunlight will do your body good. So will a little human interaction.

Finally, and this is a biggie, I apologize for my oft-quoted vision of 'a computer on every desk and in every home, all running Microsoft software.' Looking back, I realize we were doing just fine with typewriters, carbon paper, and Post-It notes. Deadlines were achieved, the stock market still hummed along and children didn't learn by saying, 'I'll just look it up online.' In a 1994 Playboy interview, I alluded to doing some mind altering substances while at Harvard. Perhaps I should have taken the high road and just said 'no.' Drugs make you do strange things. Like talk to a paperclip.

Yes, the world still waits for that confession, even as we continue purchasing reincarnates of Windows. Meanwhile, Gates retired as Microsoft CEO in 2008, retreated to his Seattle home and now, with his wife Melinda, spends every waking moment trying to rid himself of his enormous wealth, leaving only enough for a daily Starbucks. Gates has donated upwards of $25 billion for global health causes and at least $5 billion in restaurant tips.

While we remain addicted to Microsoft software in spite of the fact that using it not only makes Gates richer, but will also cause our teeth to fall out precisely on our 70th birthdays (Microsoft Terms of Use, Paragraph 465, Section 95, Subsection 1955.v), we also can't stop using Apple products, thanks to the genius of another, now departed billionaire…

Steve Jobs

While Gates famously envisioned "a computer on every desk and in every home," Jobs conversely foresaw "white buds in every pair of ears." Gates and Jobs were, at various times, partners, bitter rivals and, later, confidants due to the fact that Jobs needed Gates' help to master Microsoft Excel while Gates couldn't figure out how to create an iTunes playlist without consulting Jobs. Prior to entering the "I-everything" business, Jobs strove to make a computer simple enough for a chimpanzee—and Gates—to use. After succeeding, Jobs confused everybody by announcing the computer's creation via an unexplainable 1984 Super Bowl commercial featuring actual chimps.[26] Still, users bought the computer, dubbed "The Macintosh," because it was so much fun to drag unnecessary files into a garbage can icon that actually bulged.

Apple's board of directors were so enthralled with Jobs' world-changing product that they did what any responsible company board of directors would do: They fired him. Jobs bounced around for a few years, pouring his money into other ventures, most notably Pixar, a company renowned for making movies that toddlers and preschool-age children watch on DVD whenever their parents need a glass of wine, a small hit of marijuana, a brief moment of peace or all three. Jobs also spent his downtime realizing milk crates were not the ideal storage method for his collection of 33 1/3 albums. "What if…," Jobs asked to no one in

---

26 The spot remained the weirdest Super Bowl commercial until 2015, when Nationwide Insurance used a dead kid to narrate an ad

particular, every record album, CD, cassette, and eight track could be condensed into mp3 files and stored on a portable device?"

On October 23, 2001, back at the helm of Apple, Jobs unveiled the iPod to a room full of skeptical journalists who suddenly did an about face on the product's merits after realizing they would be receiving one for free. Their reviews were glowing: "It's small enough to carry! Small enough to jog with! Small enough to inadvertently leave on United Flight 1759 between Toronto and Chicago, thereby depriving one particular owner of EVERY PIECE OF MUSIC HE HAD ACCUMULATED SINCE HIGH SCHOOL SINCE HE FAILED TO READ THE IPOD MANUAL SECTION ENTITLED, "HOW TO BACK UP FILES!!!!""

Once Jobs realized the world's population would just purchase a replacement iPod if they lost their original one, he set about seeing if it would be possible to invent another device that, if lost, would wreak even more havoc on the consumer. Enter the iPhone and, later, the iPad. Instead of losing just your music collection, Jobs made it possible to lose contacts, photos, and videos of your wedding. He also added apps, which remind us how fat we are and when it's time to pay the mortgage. If we neglect to do the latter, the app sends us a text message, with an accompanying photo, alerting us that all our belongings are now curbside and will remain there because we are too fat to lift them.

To coincide with the iPod's release in 2001, Jobs also launched The Apple Store, a retail outlet where customers could get their Apple product-related questions answered, as opposed to waiting outside Jobs' Northern California home and shouting questions as he drove to work. In 2014, there were more than 400 Apple stores worldwide, all staffed by individuals who, judging by their demeanor, share Jobs' affinity for dropping acid. The three most chemically imbalanced employees compose "The Genius Bar." Genius Bar employees' responsibilities are threefold:

» Examine customers' allegedly broken Apple products.

» Make condescending comments.

» Reveal that the product will work fine if the user swipes the screen with his ring finger as opposed to his index finger.

By law, every Apple product owner must make at least one Genius Bar visit per year. A typical Genius Bar waiting area might contain a toddler and a 110 year old with similar iPad questions. And the line will always contain your parents.

I have never seen an Apple store back office, stock room, or break area but am convinced that a grainy, black-and-white photo of my mother, taken with an overhead security camera, adorns every bulletin board, complete with the following text:

"WARNING: 78-year-old female may enter store. Considered armed (with iPad) and extremely frustrated. Avoid eye contact but, if engaged, approach with caution. Suspect will repeatedly insist iPad is 'broken.' Carefully disarm suspect from iPad and show her how to reboot the device, as this works 99.9 percent of the time. Good luck!"

I have only myself to blame for my mother's, "There she is! Everybody look busy," label, for it was me who purchased the iPad for her and my 80-year-old father. In hindsight, I should have started with something simpler. Placing an iPad into the hands of a couple who still own a typewriter is akin to explaining the merits of digital printing to a group of Neanderthals while they create cave drawings.

I did all that I could to transition my folks into the glorious world of Apple, setting up a home network and installing a router, all without defining the purpose of either[27]. Instead, I explained the router in the same vein my parents used to explain the liquor cabinet to my sister and me when we were teenagers.

"Neither of you has any business going near this!"

I decorated their home screen with a photo of their grandchildren, and downloaded apps suitable to their tastes—Words with Friends, Sudoku,

---

27   When introducing technology to octogenarians, keep the tech talk to a minimum

The Wall Street Journal, Guess the Phrase—while extolling the virtues of portability and convenience.

"You can even watch TV on it! Now you don't have to go downstairs if your knees are acting up!"

Then, I revealed the Genius Bar's existence.

"If you ever have a question, just take the iPad to any Genius Bar," I told mom. "They will be happy to help."

This was like saying workers at the state lottery office would be perfectly willing to alter losing tickets to match the weekly Powerball numbers. Mom has made so many visits to the Genius Bar that I'm sure Apple has considered giving her "Norm from *Cheers* status," complete with her own stool. When Genius Bar employees see her enter the store, they immediately glance at their watches and decide it's time for a cigarette break, even if they don't smoke. Those who aren't fast enough face a blizzard of questions ranging from, "I pressed 'Shuffle' on my Words with Friends game, and the letters didn't move. Why is that?" to "The screen on my stock market app isn't updating. How come?" The Genius Bar employees, through their drug-induced haze, are always kind and helpful, never once replying with truthful answers like, "It's Sunday. The markets are closed, ma'am."

Finally, I decided to perform an intervention per se, anything to keep her from bellying up to the bar on a regular basis.

"Mom," I said gently, "The Genius Bar is for more, um, serious inquiries. Like, 'How come my iPad doesn't recognize any networks?' or 'How come it keeps shutting down even though the battery says 100 percent?' That sort of thing."

"You're saying my questions aren't worthy of their time?"

"I'm just saying that, 'This recipe I downloaded from the Weber Grills app doesn't taste right. How come?' may not qualify as an appropriate Genius Bar question.

"Easy for you to say. You didn't ruin two perfectly good strip steaks."

"Why don't you and Dad bounce questions off me first? If I can't answer them, then by all means, go to the Genius Bar," I said.

"Fine. How come when I press the 'mail' button, nothing happens?"

"Because you have to set up an email account. I can do that for you."

"And your father and I want to get on Facebook."

"I wouldn't do that, Mom. Facebook can be a bit overwhelming. And confusing."

"Well, if I have a question, I'll just call the Facebook offices. I'm sure they can help."

The mere mention of Facebook sent chills down my spine for, opening a Facebook account would put her at the mercy of another modern day billionaire…

Mark Zuckerberg

Known as "The Billionaire Who Has Never Visited a Clothing Store," Zuckerberg, from his Harvard dorm room in 2003, realized the world needed an outlet for sharing cat videos, vitriolic political rants, and photos of their most recent meals. When Facebook went public on May 18, 2012, Zuckerberg's net worth rose from $255.49 to $19 billion. Zuckerberg celebrated his newfound wealth by splurging on two brand new hoodies from The Gap.

At its peak, more than 1 billion individuals—approximately one-seventh of the world's total population —were using Facebook when they should have been doing just about anything else. While Facebook was originally created as a simple time waster among consumers, it soon became an awesome time waster for business. Large corporations, attracted by the idea of a billion eyeballs, launched Facebook campaigns, created Facebook pages and invited customers to click "like," falsely believing that "likes" equaled "profits." Customers who clicked "like" on the first day received a 10 percent off coupon for a Zuckerberg-autographed hoodie.

Alas, Facebook's popularity has slowly been declining. Social media experts feel this is for two reasons:

1. The parents of college students opened their own Facebook accounts and suddenly were able to view hundreds of images and video clips of their sons and daughters doing bong hits and coke lines in the student union.

2. Much to Zuckerberg's dismay, Facebook users began posting personal health updates.

The overwhelming desire to post explicit details of one's illness is the primary reason I threaten to boycott Facebook every cold and flu season. Instead, I offer to help the Center for Disease Control track how widespread the influenza virus is by reading my friends' symptoms on Facebook and reporting their geographic locations. Examples from one particularly bad flu year:

"Nose is still stuffy and now I'm coughing up phlegm." (California)

"Did somebody turn my skin inside out? It hurts to type." (Connecticut)

"Fever is currently 102.3. It's gone up a degree since yesterday. Maybe it's time to call a doctor?" (Florida)

Yes, by all means call the doctor. Better yet, VISIT the doctor. Just do something, anything, to keep you from taking photos of your current medications and posting them on your Facebook wall, as one of my New York City friends did while battling a bout of flu. Not knowing how to respond, I did what any concerned individual would do when learning about someone's flu diagnosis on Facebook: I snapped a photo of chicken soup and posted it on her wall. Facebook makes it soooooo easy!

Don't get me wrong. I'm sympathetic to those suffering from flu, as I've had the bug before and know that, as a frequent business traveler, I'm probably one airline passenger, hotel room, or subway pole away from catching the disease. But other than my immediate family or my physician, does anybody really need to know the severity of my night sweats or the side effects I endured when I took Nyquil? For the record, the latter could make you feel "really, really dizzy, like I'm flying through a tunnel with no way out." Thanks for that post, Arizona!

I do have several Facebook friends who have suffered from serious conditions—breast cancer and a brain tumor just to name two—and have read with interest the blogs, posts, and updates about their health battles. However, with rare exceptions, the flu is not a serious illness. Rather, it's a nuisance that eventually goes away and will probably disappear faster if its victims take naps instead of spending hours attempting to change their Facebook status from "married" to "feel like dog poo."

During the 2012 election season, I actually unfriended several people from my Facebook community, for I had grown weary of reading their constant, vicious political rants about both presidential candidates. Other friends I kept but blocked their posts from my wall until all the votes were tallied. I have contemplated doing the same with my flu-ridden friends, but that seems a bit harsh. It's not nice to kick people when they're down, particularly when they have a sore throat that "feels like I swallowed a case of razor blades." (Oregon)

So I continue to use Facebook, click on ads and further line Zuckerberg's hoodie pockets for he has invented a product that I find irresistible and convenient, much like the final renowned tech pioneer billionaire...

Jeff Bezos

Known in billionaire circles as "the guy who controls everything in Seattle not controlled by Bill Gates," Bezos founded Amazon.com in 1994 while driving cross country from New York City to Washington State. During the entire ride, he kept repeating, "What if I sold products to people who, if they weren't satisfied, had no idea where to return them?" Bezos' travel companion reportedly flung open the passenger door somewhere around Cleveland, Ohio and hurled himself onto the interstate to get away from Bezos' repetitiveness. But behold! Online commerce was born.

Bezos' business model was simple: Build warehouses around the country and stock them with every known commodity including commercial jets, all of which can be purchased with an Amazon Prime account and include free shipping providing the buyer is home to sign for the jet when it lands in the backyard. Like Gates and Jobs, Bezos also succeeded at revitalizing something that nobody really asked to have updated. In Gates' case Microsoft software meant we no longer needed typewriters even though they worked just fine. Jobs phased out the music CD by allowing everyone to cram their entire music collections into an iPod. Bezos one day decided that libraries were a waste of space, seeing that they contained printed books and why did we still need something that had been around since the 11th century? Enter the Amazon Kindle, a tablet device that transformed an author's printed word into that same author's digital word. Even in its original version, launched JUST IN TIME FOR CHRISTMAS 2007, the Kindle could hold approximately 200 books, never mind that the average person reads only three books in a lifetime, one of which is a John Grisham novel inadvertently left on a beach chair before the owner finished it.

Once Amazon became THE website to visit if one wanted to read, Bezos decided it should also be the website to visit if one wanted to eat, sleep, travel, or breathe (check out the sleep apnea face mask for $74.99 plus FREE SHIPPING). Today Amazon sells more than 200 million products, all of which can easily be erroneously shipped to a remote jungle in South America on December 23rd. Other retail outlets, realizing the success of online shopping, quickly followed Bezos' lead, and also began shipping orders to incorrect addresses until finally, all retail establishments got together and created a secret island void of a human populace, but littered with cardboard UPS boxes, puffy FedEx mailer envelopes, and baskets stuffed with now inedible Christmas cookies.

Bezos is also the only modern billionaire whose vision combines ecommerce with sophisticated weaponry. In 2013, during a *60 Minutes* interview, Bezos casually mentioned how his company was testing drone aircraft to deliver products to customers' front doors. Adopting the Domino's Pizza model, Bezos promised the products would be delivered in 30 minutes or less. Mind you these drone aircraft are identical to those that shoot missiles at bad guys in Afghanistan, Pakistan and other countries that despise the technology-savvy United States. Bezos insists the technology will be up and running as soon as the Department of Defense can guarantee its drone aircraft missions and Amazon aircraft deliveries will be kept separate. This potential hiccup was realized during a test mission in mid-2014 when a New Hampshire grandmother, expecting to receive a cross-stitching kit from Amazon, instead had her house obliterated by an AGM-114 Hellfire missile.

On September 17, 2011, Americans decided they were fed up with the ever widening gap between the middle class and corporate billionaires such as the four mentioned in this chapter. Armed with yoga mats and trail mix, thousands of protesters took over New York City's Zuccotti Park, calling themselves the Occupy Wall Street movement. They spent the next two months encamped in the park, passing their time typing emails on Microsoft powered laptops, ordering reinforcements on Amazon, taking thousands of photos on Apple iPhones, and uploading them all to Facebook.

The movement was called off once the group realized the extreme irony of the situation.

VI

How to Spend $3 million in Three Days (or $3.5 million if you play golf)

To: *Top Performing Managers*

Subject: *Annual Convention*

You are cordially invited to attend SYNERGY ROCKS!, our annual procurement conference and training symposium featuring TIPS AND STRATEGIES for making YOUR business more SYNERGISTIC! Held over three days at the WORLD FAMOUS MGM Resort and Casino in DYNAMIC Las Vegas, this information-packed program offers EVERYTHING. NETWORK with more than 2,500 of your fellow managers. Hear WORLD RENOWNED keynote speakers including Bangalore, India's own Dhavlip Estermonidioprakathanaqewvb, considered one of the world's leading experts on BRAND IDENTITY! Participate in scintillating ROUNDTABLE DISCUSSIONS on Six Sigma methodology. Learn to make your emails stand out by resting your elbows on the CAPS LOCK key! And get ready to

PARTY at the closing night Hawaiian themed bash. Get there a day early and participate in the pre-event GOLF TOURNAMENT. Click HERE to see (highly edited) video of last year's conference; click HERE for discounted early bird registration. Pack your HULA SKIRT and mark your CALENDAR!

Every year at a pre-determined time, higher-ups from large corporations/associations decide their respective employees/members would be more productive and think more "business-y" thoughts if they had a change of scenery, preferably one with palm trees, sunny beaches, private golf courses, casinos laden with young, single women, or all of the above.

Suffice it to say, South Dakota will never host a business convention.

If it weren't for offsite business meetings, Motel 6 would reign as the nation's most profitable hotel chain. But once word leaked that corporate America likes to exit its sterile, cubicle-laden confines at least once a year, behemoths like Mandalay Bay in Las Vegas and Gaylord Opryland in Nashville sprang up, hiring corporate event directors who sit at their desks and are highly trained not to hyperventilate from excitement when the phone rings and the voice on the other end casually says, "I'd like 1,900 rooms next January. Can you make that happen?"

According to the Convention Industry Council, 225 million people annually attend 1.8 million conventions, business meetings, corporate incentive trips and tradeshows, resulting in $115 billion to the U.S. Gross Domestic Product. [28] After enjoying staggering growth in the spend-happy 1990s and early 2000s, the meeting industry took a major hit in 2008 when it was revealed that insurance giant AIG, fresh off receiving $182 billion in federal bailout funds, (and later suing the government for its generosity), had somehow found enough loose change in its executive's pockets—$443,000 to be exact—to wine and dine its top tier insurance agents at the five-star St. Regis Resort Monarch Beach in Dana Point, California. I have stayed at this resort and came away thinking that, biblically speaking, St. Regis was the patron saint of tipping.

---

28   http://www.conventionindustry.org/ResearchInfo/EconomicSignificanceStudy/ESSKeyFindings.aspx

---

Reaction, naturally, was swift. AIG became the poster child for frivolous spending, briefly replacing the Kardashian family. Barack Obama, freshly installed as President, even jumped into the fray, singling out Las Vegas as a persona non grata destination when it came to meetings. Naturally, the outcry from the corporate travel industry was tremendous, but the president stood firm, even winning re-election four years later despite losing the all-important "Vegas cab driver" and "Vegas pole dancer" vote.

The "AIG effect," as it came to be known, caused thousands of corporate meeting planners to cancel similar events, opting instead for a night of karaoke at Slugger's Sports Bar and Grill with the year's top salesperson receiving a used iPod purchased that morning from Groupon. Eventually the economy picked up just enough steam to allow corporate meetings to return, buoyed by promises from meeting planners that they would no longer hire U2 to play during a cocktail reception for 30 software engineers. Ditto for plans to not only reserve Disney World for an evening, but also look the other way while the company CEO and his wife borrowed the Prince Charming and Cinderella costumes respectively and had sex in the castle overlooking Main Street.

Meeting planners, incidentally, are the cogs in the corporate meeting wheel. They are typically female, late 30s to early 40s, with a resume that includes "most successful cupcake mom in PS 232" and "Social chairman, Pi Beta Phi sorority, Indiana University, responsible for organizing annual 'Pimp and Slut' costume party, with all proceeds going to breast cancer awareness." Yes, planning special events is in their blood.

The planner is the first to arrive, the last to leave and the one constantly on a cell phone staring at text messages ranging from "what happened to my reservation?" to "apparently you didn't receive the email stating the CIO had a deadly shellfish allergy. Please call the morgue." The meeting planner knew this never-ending stream of crises would be part of her job duties, as evidenced by the one and only question that accompanied the interview:

"Do you wish to have an ulcer by the time you hit 30?"

If the answer is "yes", "what's an ulcer?", or "as long as I have health benefits", the meeting planner is immediately hired, assigned a cubicle and told to coordinate a 1,200-person event that the previous meeting planner had been working on before she resigned citing "stress-related issues." The event, incidentally, begins in four days.

Meeting planners exert 24-hour cheerfulness, even in the midst of a MAJOR meeting planner crisis like lack of cream cheese for the morning breakfast bagel service. They have a single mindedness and a determination to get things right; if that means donning an apron and kneading bagel dough in their hotel rooms at 3 a.m., so be it. I once eavesdropped on a planner screaming animatedly into her ever present cell phone: "These aren't the flowers for the centerpieces that I ordered. Go to a funeral if you have to; just get me the right flowers!!" Down girl!

In spite of the planner's best efforts to assemble a one of a kind, never been done before, will be talked about until the year 3000 meeting, fact is, most meetings have a "been there, done that" feel to them unless U2 actually appear. The only difference is the group having the event. The clientele may be employees from one particular company while other meetings are affairs for customers, partners, and clients. Trade associations host meetings and invite members to spend three days learning what's new in the world of vulcanized rubber. Every trade or profession has an association and therefore, an excuse to host an annual meeting. Some favorite groups whose existence I've discovered over the years include the National Funeral Directors Association ("we couldn't order liquor fast enough," according to a college buddy who once provided catering services for their Chicago soiree), the Coal Mine Methane Conference (Don't miss the always informative Black Lung breakout session!), the National United Church Usher's Association of America (Come see BIG changes in plate passing technology!), the International Association of Pet Cemeteries and Crematories (Hear ways to dispose of your parakeet in multiple languages!), the Elvis Impersonator Convention (young Elvis and fat, drug-addicted Elvis are equally represented!) and my personal favorite, the Gentlemen's Club Owner's Expo, which meets yearly in, you guessed it, Rapid City, South Dakota!

Only kidding. It's Vegas of course. In an industry that requires looking at naked women writhing on stage 10 hours a day, I can only assume that these guys come to Sin City and search out a bowling alley or a movie theatre. Whatever it takes to get away from the office.

Prior to the AIG debacle, business conventions made news for reasons other than gargantuan spending. In 1976, a group of American Legion members meeting in Philadelphia came down with a mysterious illness, with symptoms including fever, chills, muscle aches, vomiting, and a desire to wear funny hats. Their illness came to be known as Legionnaires Disease. No cure has been found for either the malady or the poor fashion choices.

Continuing the death theme, in 2004, McDonald's CEO Jim Cantalupo suffered a fatal heart attack in his hotel room, just hours before he was to address a ballroom full of McDonald's owner/operators. The always sympathetic press used that incident to pepper surviving McDonald's executives with Cantalupo's eating habits, i.e. did the McDonald's menu contribute to his demise? The restaurant chain's top brass danced around the question, but did announce that sales of Double Quarter Pounders with cheese remained stronger than ever. Ditto for Super Size fries.

In 2010, former Hewlett-Packard CEO Mark Hurd abruptly resigned after alleged inappropriate behavior with a female who worked as a "hostess" at several HP off-site events. That same year, taxpayers footed an $823,000 bill for a three-day General Services Administration junket. Among the expenditures for a government agency charged with managing office leases and properties: a mind reader and a clown. While the mind reader expense was overlooked, federal investigators said there were plenty of clowns in Washington who would have performed the gig for expenses only.

Such indiscretions are the reason watchdog agencies are now constantly on the lookout for any group that dares to spend more than $3.89 on anything convention related, even a plane ticket. Indeed, during the dark years of 2009-2011—known in the meeting world as, "Doing More with Less...Or Nothing at All,"— many companies considered the idea of hosting "virtual" meetings. By this time, technology had grown sophisticated enough to allow hundreds, even thousands of meeting attendees to log onto a secure website and, from the privacy of their home offices, hear all the speeches and get all the information that they would have received had they flown to Palm Springs. "Think of the savings in airfare," meeting planners shrieked. "Think of the convenience. Think of the novelty!"

What they didn't think about is that the average attention span of a home office worker watching a webcast is about 14 seconds, not counting the eight seconds spent running to the refrigerator for a yogurt. Also, it didn't help that all the speakers were clothed in golf shirts, sandals, and sun block, leading the attendees to believe, correctly, that the executives were conducting the webcast from an exotic Caribbean destination while everybody else logged in from Eau Claire, Wisconsin in mid-January.

Which is why the offsite meeting will always endure, even after all U2 members have died. If you have any desire to attend one, let me provide you with the template. Start with the...

MEETING INVITATION

Meeting invitations are distributed three to six months before the actual event as meeting organizers know potential attendees need this much time to gently inform their spouses that they will be away at a "mandatory business conference" which, coincidentally, occurs the same week as their child's youth soccer tournament, parent-teacher get together, high school midterms, and the annual Neighborhood Clean Up event. The attendee apologizes profusely, but reminds the spouse again that attendance is mandatory. So is the golf tournament.

Invites are distributed via email and usually contain a photograph or video clip that is flagged by company filters, causing the invite to be dumped into the invitee's spam folder. Millions of company employees are currently sitting at their desks in quarter-filled offices wondering why everybody else is calling in from Sonoma, California. Eventually they search their junk boxes and, to their chagrin, realize they were invited to an all-expenses-paid conference featuring a seminar entitled, "How Drinking Five Glasses of Merlot a Day Can Increase Your Productivity!"

For those who do locate the invitation and RSVP, the event actually begins a day early, as every meeting, convention, et al. must include a ...

TRAVEL DAY

Attendees use this day to fly from wherever to the meeting destination. One third of these flights will be cancelled and another third will be delayed by at least four hours, causing the meeting planner to reluctantly tell the hotel staff that the, "RESERVED FOR PRIVATE EVENT," sign at the pool's entrance can be removed and all the non-meeting hotel guests can go swimming after all. Those attendees who are fortunate enough to reach their destination are escorted, via private shuttle bus, to the hotel, where they wander over to the registration area and are given a "welcome bag" containing literature from sponsoring organizations and two individually wrapped breath mints. They also receive a name badge clipped to a lanyard adorned with another sponsor logo. Ninety percent of meeting attendees keep this badge around their necks for the next three days, never removing it, even when showering. I once observed a Vegas (naturally) meeting attendee who, six hours after the dinner banquet had ended, was leaning over a craps table, badge dangling directly in the playing area. A pair of dice from another player actually hit the badge before landing on the table, producing a pair of fours or a "hard eight," if you are one of the world's 26 people who understands craps. The pit boss declared the throw illegal. The badge wearer, instead of taking off his nametag, merely tossed it over his shoulder and placed another ten dollar chip on the come line. The other players looked as if they wanted to inflict serious harm on him and, thanks to his badge, were able to threaten him by first, last and company name.

Once all attendees have received their nametags, they cool their heels for a few hours until it's time for the...

OPENING NIGHT RECEPTION!

Also known as "the first event with open bar," the kickoff to the frivolity begins poolside, with elaborate decorations and themes that force hotel workers to dress in the practical (tropical) to the ridiculous (a Filipino busboy in a New England Patriots jersey to coincide with the "Super Bowl" theme just doesn't look right.) Cocktails flow, hors d'oeuvres are replenished and attendees commence the first round of "networking," the business term for "uncomfortable small talk." "Paradigm shift" notwithstanding, "network," and forms thereof is the most overused word in today's business environment. The opening night "NETWORKING" reception gives way to the next day's "NETWORKING" lunch and the chance to "NETWORK" with company leaders. Let's not forget the "NETWORKING" bathroom break (gentlemen, you never know who may be urinating next to you), the "NETWORKING" elevator ride back to your room, the "NETWORKING" cocktail reception, the "NETWORKING" dinner, and late night "NETWORKING" in the hotel bar, which can lead to "CASUAL NETWORKING SEX". After two days of this, attendees are pleading with the meeting planner to organize a "GET THE HELL AWAY FROM ME" breakfast.

The party usually breaks up around 1 a.m., though last call really should have been three hours earlier. The patrons stumble to their rooms, knowing they have precious little time to sleep off their oncoming hangovers because at precisely 8 a.m., it's time for the...

OPENING GENERAL SESSION!!

Bleary-eyed attendees enter a massive hotel ballroom, where workers had, just hours ago, finished arranging chairs in perfectly synchronized rows under the watchful eyes of the meeting planner. The meeting participants quickly fill up the hinter most rows and whip out their iPads or copies of *USA Today*, both necessary items when enduring an opening general session. A giant stage, flanked by two video screens that I would kill to have in my house, is empty but powerful speakers blare "walk in" music, reflecting the event's positive theme. Popular choices over the years have been The Rolling Stones', "Start Me Up," the Black Eyed Peas', "Let's Get It Started," and Owl City's, "Good Time." During the meltdown of 2008-9, Bon Jovi's, "Livin' on a Prayer" received a lot of spins.

Once seated, the president of the company or association sponsoring the meeting takes the stage and spends between 20 and 45 minutes proving that company presidents are ghastly public speakers. Normally if a president or CEO starts speaking at 9 a.m. attendees will casually begin scrolling through their phones at 9:02. Once all emails are read, text messages begin to materialize from attendees seated at opposite ends of the room.

EMPLOYEE 1: How long do u think this guy will drone on?

EMPLOYEE 2: IHNFI

EMPLOYEE 1: ???

EMPLOYEE 2: I have no f-----g idea. Sorry

EMPLOYEE 1: NPITOBT?

EMPLOYEE 2: ???

EMPLOYEE 1: No problem. Is there open bar tonight?

CEOs ALWAYS speak over their allotted time, prompting consternation from the meeting planner, who has carefully scripted the session down to the second. I was once told to perform from 8:36 a.m. to 8:43 a.m., "but if they're really laughing hard, you can go to 8:44." Even more infuriating is that the CEO, at various intervals, teases the audience into thinking he is actually wrapping up his speech by inserting phrases such as, "in conclusion," "summing it up," and "my final thought," only to draw silent groans from everybody in attendance by inevitably saying, "Can we go back a slide please?"

The "slide" refers to PowerPoint, a Microsoft product that singlehandedly extended the life of a speech threefold and is the reason the lavish video screens had to be rented for $3,000 a day. Prior to PowerPoint's creation, speakers were forced to walk on stage armed with nothing more than a lavaliere microphone and an overwhelming fear of failure. If the speaker forgot a major chunk of his speech, there were no visual cues letting him know that, yes, he skipped over the part about the company's upcoming Chapter 11 filing and the layoffs that would result. PowerPoint allows him to beautifully illustrate the announcement, complete with slides featuring a blood red background, (for bankruptcy), and numerous stick figures whose heads are being separated from their bodies with a clipart chainsaw. If the company is, in any way involved in technology, the presentation will also include numerous unintelligible diagrams with arrows jutting in every direction and little boxes identified as "servers" with lightning bolts protruding from them, giving the impression that whatever is illustrated in the slide is powering not only this country, but surrounding countries as well.

PowerPoint has become such a crutch in the business world that it's only a matter of time before it makes its way into the home environment.

HUSBAND: Honey, I'm home. What's for dinner?

WIFE: What's for dinner? Dim the lights and I'll tell you what's for dinner.

(VIDEO SCREEN DESCENDS FROM CEILING. WIFE BEGINS TO NARRATE)

WIFE: Let's begin with slide one, my mission statement. As you can see, it reads, "Initiate a meal action plan consisting of a nutritional, well-balanced menu for two adults and two children while staying within the confines of a household budget and leaving room for expenditures including college tuition, retirement funds and yearly vacations. Form a synergistic alliance between this duty and my other functions without causing a paradigm shift and losing my meal empowerment abilities.

HUSBAND: Honey, wait…

WIFE: Next slide please. (CLICK) The blue line represents the amount of groceries that should be in the refrigerator while the red line represents all the other crap I had to do today. The precise intersection of those lines signals the moment I realized I had to be three places at once and not one of them was the grocery store.

HUSBAND: Seriously honey, you don't have to…

WIFE: NEXT SLIDE PLEASE. (CLICK) Now here's an interesting slide. Here is a topographical photo, obtained from Google Maps, which shows our neighborhood and the surrounding business district. Recognize it? Now let me add these colored dots (CLICK) each of which represents a fast-food establishment within three miles of our house.

HUSBAND: Are you mad at me?

WIFE: Which leads to my final slide… (CLICK)…my new company slogan: "Get off your back. Get a Big Mac." I will now take questions.

Eventually the welcome speeches subside, at which point it's time to release the masses into...

BREAKOUT SESSIONS!

"Breakout" is a very misleading term as it implies that something positive will come from sitting in a windowless meeting room surrounded by movable partitions. Need three rooms for 100 people as opposed to one room for 300? No worries. Just press a button, (or get a bunch of burly hotel workers to pull the partition by hand), and a hotel is reconfigured right in front of you. The rooms are soundproof which is necessary so when participants in, "Increasing Operational Efficiencies with an Open Database Connectivity Interface," end their session early and exit the room, the attendees still stuck in, "Complete A-Z for 753R Wireless Remote Telemetry Solutions,"[29] can't hear them outside.

At various times throughout the day, the attendees will come up for air through a series of quick breaks known as, (Surprise!), "NETWORKING opportunities." Instead of doing what they really want to do, namely retreat to their hotel rooms and watch a few more minutes of the pay-per-view porn movie they had to pause because it was time to head down to the opening session, the attendees sip Diet Coke, eat granola bars, and begin every conversation with, "So what did you think?" All information gleaned from these networking chats will be promptly forgotten within five minutes.

As the afternoon stretches onward, a buzz begins to fill the halls for attendees know that they will soon reconvene in the main ballroom just in time to hear the...

MOTIVATIONAL SPEAKER!

Just in case the CEO and his sizzling PowerPoint slides weren't enough to shoot adrenaline through the veins of every meeting attendee, an outside speaker is brought in, guaranteed to help boost sales and company morale providing every attendee purchases the speaker's latest book and 8-disc DVD set. The motivational speaker is a curious breed; every time I talk to one, I eventually find myself thinking, "Nobody can be this positive. Doesn't he ever wake up and say, "my life sucks?""

Incidentally, motivational speakers even have their own association and, consequently, their own meeting. Held once a year, the National

---

29   Titles from an actual meeting. I swear!

Speaker's Association conference features a hotel full of people walking around trying to motivate each other. Listening to them is sort of like being repeatedly hit in the head with a rubber mallet; it doesn't hurt, but your brain slowly goes numb.

Motivational speakers can be easily divided into three categories: The first is the ex-athlete, coach, politician, or outrageously successful businessperson who actually has motivated his or her charges by leading a team to a World Series title, winning a war, or taking a floundering company and turning it around. These speakers are household names and command price tags and perks representative of their notoriety. Former President George W. Bush requires a private jet to shuttle him to speeches so he can tell a room full of business leaders how they too can plunder an economy by looking the opposite direction while banks write mortgages for first time homebuyers who answered "14 cents" when asked to estimate their net worth's. These "A list" speakers have told the same stories thousands of times, but audiences are still enthralled because the guy who just a few short years ago was heaving the winning Super Bowl pass is now 50 feet away and willing to pose for selfies with anybody who asks.

At a significantly lower price tag are the ex-jocks who had their moment of glory, but have since faded into oblivion and must therefore bring video clips of their athletic feats so the audience can think, "Oh yeah, I remember this guy. Sort of." Better yet, some will actually exhibit their athletic skills directly on stage. I once saw an Olympic gold-medal-winning pommel horse athlete perform a few scissors kicks on the apparatus, which I assume had to be ordered specifically as most hotels do not have gymnastics equipment lying around. However, the GSA may have one in storage from its 2010 convention. No doubt the meeting planner had to work magic once she read the speaker's performance rider and saw the following: "Speaker requires one pot of black coffee backstage, one bottle of water onstage and one pommel horse center stage." While the gymnast's routine was impressive, I failed to realize what it had to do with increasing sales. Most of the attendees looked as if they could barely do a pushup, much less a double leg circle.

The second category of motivational speakers are those who have stared death in the face and lived to tell about it. Whether it's trudging down Mt. Everest after being abandoned during a blizzard[30], cutting off an appendage after it was trapped by a boulder while hiking[31], or being shot down during a routine mission over Afghanistan[32], these speakers, through riveting video clips and horrifying first person accounts, eventually depress the entire audience into thinking, "Wow, what a loser I am. All I've done is sell term life insurance." Still these types of speakers are my favorites because their stories stick with the attendees and are often retold at other meeting events, sometimes inappropriately. NOTE: The company awards dinner is not the place to casually say, "So Ted, if this entire table was in a plane crash and you were the only survivor, which one of us would you eat first?"

Now we come to the third and most positively annoying motivational speaker. They are not famous, have not endured tragedy, and have probably been fired from several jobs in their lifetimes. What they do possess is the ability to take a five-minute story and turn it into a 45-minute story while being so continually positive and upbeat that they may have future careers as meeting planners. They coin catchphrases such as, "I'm feeling F-F-F-Fantastic!" and repeat the phrase ad nauseum, just to make sure their 45 minutes are covered. Those who lack phrases seek out audience participation. I once witnessed a speaker tell the audience to form a perimeter around the room. He then instructed them to clasp hands one by one, (think "The Wave" with less effort), until eventually everybody would be holding hands and silently craving anti-bacterial lotion. While men held hands with other men, the speaker earned $10,000 by timing them with a stopwatch. He then announced that they needed to do it again and this time, cheer each other on. Again, what this has to do with

30   Dr. Beck Weathers
31   Aron Ralston
32   Take your pick

increasing productivity is beyond me, but the audience seemed to be enjoying it. After four or five tries, the speaker seemed satisfied and was left with a few minutes to hawk his DVDs.

Opening speeches, breakout sessions and motivation are the hallmarks of every meeting. In between there are other activities which may or may not appear. Among those I have witnessed over the years...

SPEED NETWORKING

Just in case the attendees feel they need MORE chances to network, an hour or so is set aside for the business person's version of online dating. Attendees file into a ballroom and stand on one side of long tables that clutter the room. Vendors or other attendees stand on the other side. At the sound of a bell, quick conversations between both sides ensue. The interplay goes something like this:

SPEED NETWORKING ATTENDEE 1: Hi, I'm Stan from company ABC.

SPEED NETWORKING ATTENDEE 2: Pleased to meet you Stan. I'm Jim from company XYZ.

SPEED NETWORKING ATTENDEE 1: So what is it you guys do?

SOUND OF BELL SIGNALLING THE END OF THE FIRST ROUND

Literally that's how long attendees have to converse before moving on. I once witnessed a speed networking session between scientists in the bioprocess arena, a subject so technical that it took me 10 minutes just to pronounce the titles of some of the breakout sessions. Yet, attendees still found time to speed network with their cohorts, beginning conversations with, "I want to talk about cell culture process development, but I've only got a minute."

TEAM BUILDING ACTIVITY

Yet another way to foster networking is to divide the attendees into small groups and assign them some task that must be completed over a three-hour period. I've seen everything from "create a commercial with a FLIP camera that represents diversity in the workplace" to "build a boat using materials that the Q character in James Bond movies wouldn't even have lying around." While these events have every intention of fostering camaraderie, they invariably lead to petty infighting and jealousy among team members who can't agree on who should be elected "scavenger hunt leader."

If bickering didn't materialize during the team building affair, it will certainly erupt at the meetings' final event, also known as the...

CLOSING NIGHT AWARDS BANQUET!

The most formal event of the conference, this sit down dinner, (preceded by open bar naturally), is a chance for the organization's most valuable employees to be recognized with plaques and quickly staged photos with the organization's top brass. Categories range from the general, (Most Enthusiastic Employee), to the minute, (Top Employee with Sales Between $250,000 and $499,999 In Territories Containing At Least One State Ending In 'Y.'"). For reasons I have never been able to figure out, the most prestigious awards are handed out at the very end, much like the Oscars. Unfortunately, by this time, most audience members are either too inebriated to hear what's happening onstage or are in their rooms, packing for their early morning flights. This is why the Deep South Territory Manager of the Month receives thunderous applause while the Sales Person of the Millennium can muster only a few half-hearted golf claps.

Once all awards have been distributed and silent grumblings of, "I can't believe Joe got that award. He's such a dick," completed, there is one more order of business: Announce where next year's meeting will be held!

Dim the lights, roll the video, and watch audience members react as they glimpse images of what looks to be a shimmering ocean, but in reality is Lake Erie, which surrounds Cleveland, home of the Rock and Roll Hall of Fame. What better place to hold next year's event, announces the CEO or the meeting planner, if she is still employed. Attendees should mark their calendars now as they don't want to miss out on the event, which will feature some incredible entertainment:

An ass-kicking U2 cover band.

VII

Feeling like a King at 30,000 Feet

*TO: **Wilbur Wright***
*CC: **Orville Wright***
*FROM: **Early American Airlines***
*RE: **Frequent flyer program launch***

Dear Wright Brothers:

We are excited to inform you that, in light of your success at Kitty Hawk last weekend, we have developed a "frequent" flyer program that we trust will meet your approval.

Passengers who fly more than 100,000 miles a year on your aircraft will obtain "premium" status, allowing them special perks when flying. These may include an upgraded seat, (you are eventually going to add seats to your flying machine, correct?), an inflight snack or a free movie rental. Note: Do you think it's possible to show Charlie Chaplin's, "The Kid," on transcontinental flights? It was the top vote getter at our office!

Please continue to monitor your progress and report back to us with any new developments. Also, is there room on your plane for overhead storage? How about a lavatory?

FROM: Orville Wright
TO: Early American Airlines
RE: Your inquiry

To Whom It May Concern:

While we appreciate your enthusiasm to begin charging customers, need we remind you that our airplane only flew 105 feet yesterday? While this shows progress, we feel it's a wee bit early to begin booking revenue passengers. Wilbur nearly fell out of the cockpit which, incidentally, remains accessible to the passenger cabin and, therefore, a haven for terrorist activity. We will keep you apprised of any new developments. Right now we are devoting our energies to safety belts for passengers should they ever be allowed aboard. I have developed a contraption that involves placing a metal fitting into a buckle and strapping it securely about one's waist, but it's too complicated to explain in detail. Should this device be successful, it would most likely have to be demonstrated aboard every flight until the end of time.

I am reasonably sure that airline frequent flyer programs are the sole reasons some small countries are able to survive financially. A quiet, never-make-the-news, no-real-reason-to-go-there country, like Singapore, would be nothing more than a large, uninhabited land mass with mild temperatures were it not for U.S. business people who eagerly volunteer to jet across the International Date Line for a two hour meeting, pick up a few made-in-Singapore trinkets for the kids, and return home in time for dinner —or breakfast. After basically spending three straight days in an airplane, who cares what's on the table as long as it's soft so the weary traveler can comfortably collapse face down in it. But a face full of Jell-O or scrambled egg is a small price to pay for the privilege of obtaining top tier airline status. Just ask Ric Murray.

A veteran of the cellular network industry, the 60-something Murray is one of those travelers whose frequent flier statements look like national debt figures. Murray's fascination with travel began when he waited tables at Walt Disney World and saw large numbers of international tour groups enter the premises.

"It put the bug in me," said Murray, who once rode his bike cross country so lengthy travel trips are in his blood. His international job and the travel it entails keeps him flying, by his estimates, 300,000 miles per year. Add to that miles he collects through credit card programs and his total mileage accumulation is nearly 3 million miles on Delta Airlines and a similar figure on American, his new carrier of choice.

"When they eliminated pillows, (on Delta), I switched," he said.

Murray knows every plane's configuration, ("don't take row 15 on a 767), claims immunity to jet lag, and knows exactly what to do once he's settled into his seat.

"Two Heinekens and an Ambien and I'm out," he said.

Like most brilliant ideas that started successfully and eventually were tweaked just enough to turn them into public relations disasters, the concept of rewarding customers for airline loyalty began in the late 1970s. Both United and American claim invention of the frequent flyer program. Other airlines followed suit and today, airline travel has turned into a no-holds-barred competition, complete with a class system not seen since slaves toiled in Confederate cotton fields. Were Thomas Jefferson alive today, his signature phrase, "All men are created equal," would come with the tagline ..."until they purchase airline tickets." Airports have become a sea of red carpets, board-before-everybody-else check-in lines, and 70-pound illegal bags that suddenly become 30-pound perfectly legal bags containing drugs, liquids, and the occasional weapon solely because the bag contains a gold "One million mile flier" tag on the strap.

I began exploring frequent flyer programs once I started making enough money to ditch my red 1987 Nissan Sentra and experience the joy of leaving for, and arriving to, comedy engagements on the same day. For the first year I was happy just to tell other comedians I flew, which made them especially envious. Once, while sitting in the green room at a South Carolina club—at 95 percent of comedy clubs, "green room," is a nice way of saying, "the kitchen,"—I was bemoaning the fact that the club was 30 miles from the Greenville/Spartanburg Airport. The two other comics, who had shared a car from their previous gig in Jacksonville, Florida looked at me like I had a personal valet waiting outside to cleanse my hands with anti-bacterial soap after a meet-and-greet. It was a nice feeling.

As the airline trips piled up I began realizing, through verbal conversations and eavesdropping, that passengers were actually being REWARDED for flying, even if their flights involved having a tray table in their laps while sitting between a crying infant with a digestive disorder and a sinus-challenged octogenarian. Their reward? A chance to do the same thing for less money! Or even for free! I eagerly listened and, before long, was jetting to far flung destinations without removing my wallet, never mind that I had removed my wallet numerous times, mostly through useless credit card purchases, in order to accrue enough mileage for one lousy ticket.

Just as everybody was starting to get the hang of airline perks, two cataclysmic events changed the airline experience forever. The first occurred on September 11, 2001 when hijacked planes became weapons of mass destruction. After realizing that terrorists casually strolled through security checkpoints carrying box cutters, the Transportation Security Administration increased its screening process by forcing casual travelers to strip naked and pour large amounts of contact lens solution into buckets. True, the system isn't perfect, but TSA officials are quick to point out the process is constantly evolving and will be perfect once employees are able to identify and arrest the following passengers:

Pillow Girl. Late teens to early 20s. Wearing plaid pajama bottoms and clutching a KING-SIZED pillow that will apparently accompany her everywhere, even if her final destination is a yearlong stint aboard a submarine. Ladies, pillows are like your last boyfriend; you found one, it was nice and comfortable for a while, but there's always a better one nearby. Also remember that carrying your pillow around for a while causes it to lose its shape and become less desirable, sort of like the boyfriend you will eventually marry.

Important Call Guy. Male, 35-55, dressed in a business suit. No need for visual confirmation; just listen for the sound of someone having an animated cellphone conversation the entire time he is in line. Prone to running his phone through the X-ray machines while still connected, saying, "Hang on. Lemmee clear security and I'll get right back to you." If allowed to board, will continue talking despite repeated warnings from flight attendants to "turn it off," "shut it down," or "shove it up your nose." TSA, if spotted, pull this passenger from the line and immediately conduct a full body search. Make sure the offender's phone is nearby so the party on the other end can hear you say, "Okay, Mr. Johnson, we just need to check your anal cavity, and then you're free to go."

Bin Hog. The maximum number of bins for each passenger is two: one for a laptop and one for everything else, massive pillow included. TSA, remind anybody scooping up seven bins and delicately placing one item in each that these items will be confiscated and sold on eBay.

PSP Pubescent. Male or female. Usually 9-13. Playing PSP or Nintendo handheld video game in security line and reluctant to part with it, even for the few seconds it takes to be screened. If identified, take these children aside and calmly explain that, at their age, air travel is a privilege and would it kill them to leave the stupid game at home?

Queen and/or King of Bling. These are the most experienced security line passengers since each trip through the X-ray machine requires several additional trips before an offending piece of jewelry is found and removed. TSA screeners, if you see something, say something, preferably, "Please remove all metal objects, including navel jewelry, tongue piercings, eyebrow beads, and nipple clamps." With the possible exception of Important Call Guy, you will have everybody's attention.

Stroller Mom. Despite having successfully done so hundreds of times, forgets how to fold the stroller when approaching machine. TSA, quickly offer to assist as Stroller Dad is useless.

Just as Americans were warming to the idea of walking through a screening machine wearing nothing but socks, the financial crash of 2008 hit, sending the airline industry, and frequent flier programs in particular, into a free fall. Reward miles became useless for two reasons:

» The airline was about to go bankrupt.

» The airline already had gone bankrupt, but flights were still in the air because the maintenance department overfilled the fuel tanks and, well, we wouldn't want to jettison perfectly good jet fuel over a public park in Omaha, Nebraska now, would we?

Pilots were not averse to making Chapter 11 announcements mid-flight:

Attention ladies and gentlemen. While we have plenty of fuel to make it to San Francisco, we have just been informed that we are out of money. Therefore, we will be landing in Tulsa, Oklahoma approximately 45 seconds from now. Your frequent flyer accounts have also been terminated. If this news causes you concern, there are air sickness bags in your seat backs.

Once executives at large corporations realized the airline industry was in shambles and hitchhiking might be their only alternative for attending out-of-area business meetings, they did the only logical thing: purchased private jets for themselves with money they did not possess. This brilliant idea came under intense scrutiny during a congressional hearing on November 19, 2008 when chief executives from Ford, Chrysler, and General Motors came before the House Financial Services committee pleading for bailout funds while sheepishly admitting all took corporate jets to Washington DC that day.

"Couldn't you have downgraded to first class…or jet pooled to get here?" an exasperated Rep. Gary Ackerman (D-NY) asked. The question remains the funniest line to come out of Washington since Bill Clinton's, "I did not have sex with that woman," zinger.

Airlines that fell into the bankruptcy pit eventually extricated themselves by posting messages in the "hook up" section of Craigslist:

One multibillion dollar, financially irresponsible transportation company seeks similar for good times and stable bottom line. Owner must be okay with the title, "Co-CEO." Routes to Asia a definite plus.

The strategy worked; federal judicial panels quickly approved the mergers simply because all the judges had frequent flyer accounts and were anxious to begin using them again. American Airlines hooked up with U.S. Airways while United became buddies with Continental Airlines. Delta meshed with Northwest Airlines, acquiring the popular "flights to the frozen tundra" routes in the process.

Unfortunately all of these mergers sent frequent flier programs into a freefall of confusion and anxiety. Loyal travelers, wondering the status of their points, received letters detailing the new programs:

Dear valued customer:

Thank you for your frequent service on our airline. In the previous calendar year you accrued 112,345 miles with us. While that normally would be cause for celebration, we regret to inform you that Stephen, a businessman from Amarillo, Texas, is now flying our airline due to the merger. His 112, 346 miles just bumped you off the first class upgrade list. But don't worry; it's a brand new year!

The shaky economy also succeeded in reducing the number of carriers from "many" to "few" with American, United, Delta, and Southwest now assuming command of the skies. Gone were the days when all it took to enter the airline industry was a bank loan and a friendship with a guy who builds model planes so really, how hard can it be to build a real one? Case in point? Hooters Air. Launched in 2003, the chicken wing empire assumed, correctly for a while, that its zesty wings and scantily clad wait staff/flight attendants would be all the incentive travelers needed to fly to vacation destinations, (Myrtle Beach, Nassau), by way of horrible starting points, (Yes, that is Newark on your left). Hooters ceased operation in 2006 after a pilot, fresh off eating a dozen "Three Mile Island" wings, inadvertently rubbed his eyes, forcing the co-pilot to make an emergency landing. A fire crew met the plane and turned its hoses on the pilot's face for 45 minutes. Even though passengers were unaware of the delay—most were playing "Beer Pong" with the flight attendants—federal transportation officials pulled the airline's license.

Once the economy rebounded and airlines realized how dependent the universe was on travel via the skies, executives immediately jumped to the, sadly correct, conclusion that passengers did not need pre-financial crash perks such as meals, elbow room, and a flushable toilet. Their decision was a boondoggle for the airport restaurant industry, which immediately installed, "Grab and Go," kiosks outside their establishments. A more appropriate and factually correct title would be, "Stop and Look at What You Are Purchasing Before Grabbing and Going," but that wouldn't fit on the signs.

To boost revenue, and in turn build more planes, airlines charged customers extra fees for luxuries such as "a bag, even one that contains lifesaving medication." The newer planes contain approximately 150 more seats than the older models yet are exactly the same size. How is this possible? Technically it isn't unless one chooses to install additional rows of seats *between* the existing rows. This new method of flying with your knees resting against your chin is, nowadays, seen as perfectly normal to airlines like JetBlue which, in a highly mocked press release, proudly ANNOUNCED that it was reducing legroom on flights. While some may see that move about as dumb as Coca Cola announcing, in 1985, that it was changing its recipe, JetBlue shares actually increased on that day, proving that Americans enjoy pain and suffering.

Some American citizens did fight back, including Washington DC resident Ira Goldman who, in August 2014, caused a major stir with his invention, the Knee Defender. On a United Airlines flight between Newark and Denver, a female passenger trying to recline her coach seat was thwarted by the Knee Defender, a $21.95 simple plastic device the male passenger seated behind her had clipped to his tray table. She complained; he refused to remove it. She threw water at him and the pilot made an unscheduled landing in Chicago where both passengers were ordered to extricate themselves from the plane, no easy matter when crammed in coach.

I'm not surprised there was confrontation aboard this flight; after all it did originate in New Jersey. What shocked me was how many air travelers, through ensuing blogs and social media posts, defended Knee Defender Guy. Six foot plus individuals, laptop users, claustrophobes and, naturally, Goldman were among the most vocal. Conversely, I found myself solely in Water Throwing Girl's camp, feeling I should have the right to use whatever features come with my coach seat, limited as they are. Imagine buying a car with a top-of-the-line stereo system and stumbling across the following sentence in the owner's manual: WARNING! DRIVER WILL NOT PLAY KENNY CHESNEY ON RADIO IF ANY COUNTRY MUSIC HATER IS IN VEHICLE.

While airlines discourage the Knee Defender, it is not illegal to bring aboard, meaning frequent fliers like myself and Murray now need an offense to counter Goldman's device. Passing gas immediately comes to mind, but I have no qualm with anybody else in the row behind me. Or next to me. Or in front of me. Or across the aisle. Casually dumping a glass of red wine on the Knee Defender offender would look suspicious as it would require a 180-degree move on my part.

The most obvious answer? Speed. During takeoff, seatbacks must be in the upright position, tray tables stowed, blah, blah, blah. Once the plane is airborne, I'm positive I can recline my seat faster than the passenger behind me can assemble the Knee Defender. You snooze, you lose.

So I've solved that dilemma. And now that my brain is in full airplane problem-conquering mode, I'm always jotting down ideas that, one day, will make up my own line of commercially sold passenger defense mechanisms. For starters I will patent the Elbow Separator, a thin metal sheet that easily divides a row's community armrest. Side by side coach passengers get an equal three-quarters of an inch all the way to Hawaii.

Next comes the Shoulder Jolt, an electrically-charged cushion I'll wear behind my neck. Any sleeping passenger whose head listlessly flops onto my shoulder mid-flight gets the shock of their lives, no pun intended.

Finally, don't board without my number one creation, Foot Odor in a Jar. Put it in your pocket and discretely open it when your fellow passenger removes his shoes. The quickly intensifying smell tricks Stocking Feet Guy into thinking he is the source of the stink. Note: This product is not always needed; I've flown next to passengers whose feet smell far worse than anything produced in a lab.

Airlines, while doing nothing about improving comfort, have turned to technology to take our minds off the fact that coronary thrombosis is imminent despite the fact that there are still four hours before touchdown. For a small fee, passengers can purchase in flight Wi-Fi, giving them the freedom to text, "Guy in seat next to me won't stop farting," to friends and relatives, via their iPads. A debate continues to rage over whether in flight cell phone conversations should be allowed. Currently passengers are relegated to quick phone calls prior to take off. I often eavesdrop and have determined that the most popular topics of pre-flight conversations are, "How was soccer today, honey?" and "HOW COME STEVE NEVER

COPIED ME ON THAT F---G EMAIL?" The latter conversation is usually repeated once the plane lands, the caller checks his email and angrily realizes Steve still hasn't complied.

My carrier of choice has long been American Airlines. No real reason. I choose airlines like I choose golf clubs; if nothing tragic happens while I'm using the product, it must be okay. As my career escalated, so did my frequent flier miles until, almost by accident, I had achieved that magic number of 100,000 miles in a calendar year. Exactly how far is that? Well, take a ball of string and attach one end to a luggage cart at LAX. Begin walking east. After about 4,000 miles you would fall into the Atlantic Ocean and drown, rendering this experiment pointless. It's a lot; let's leave it at that.

In previous years I had accrued Gold status, a mere 25,000 miles. While this may seem triumphant, Gold status is sort of like strolling into a Maui hotel and announcing you are on your honeymoon and should therefore be fawned over by the staff. Hotel employees will smile politely, mutter a few Hawaiian curse words like, "ikonomonowokia,"[33] under their breath, and direct you to the special "honeymoon line," which currently contains about 300 other newlyweds, half of whom will be divorced before getting to speak to the concierge.

The next goal to fall was Platinum status or 50,000 miles. Impressive, but still nothing to brag about; kind of like earning a silver medal in the Olympics. Worse, one must double that output to reach the next rung, Executive Platinum. Thankfully, Olympic gold medal hopefuls need not abide by the same formula in order to achieve their dreams:

Jeremy, your 10.6 second 100-yard dash time was truly impressive. Think you can get it down to 5.3 seconds before the next Olympics?

American Airlines also makes it possible to become Executive Platinum by flying 120 segments in a calendar year. It's very simple: A segment is a single flight, even if that flight sits on the tarmac for three hours in January

---

33 A Hawaiian phrase meaning "Allow me to insert this pineapple in your crotch"

while a de-icing crew is located. Flying nonstop to Dallas for a meeting and returning nonstop to Chicago counts as two segments. Flying out of Chicago and connecting in Indianapolis, Omaha, Hot Springs, Arkansas, Boise, and Portland before landing in Dallas counts as six if I calculated correctly. Of course, doing so would cause the flyer to miss his meeting by two days and be fired from his job, but it would give him more time to return to Chicago via New Orleans, Miami, Bangor, Maine, and San Jose, further padding his frequent flyer segment total.

In addition to being certifiably insane, another quality "mileage chasers" like myself must possess is above average math skills. A mileage chaser's worst nightmare is realizing that it's December 30 and we have miscalculated by a few miles or one segment. This means we must purchase a same day flight to a city one could easily walk to. Airlines know our desperation and adjust their prices accordingly. A round trip ticket between Chicago and St. Louis normally costs me about $150. However, were I to book in the crunch time period leading up to a new calendar year, the fee would contain at least one comma.

And don't even try to call the airlines and plead with them to "round up" your miles, a fact I've discovered on several occasions:

ME: *Right now I'm at 99,947 miles. Can you just round that up to 100,000 please?*

FREQUENT FLYER DESK: *I'm sorry sir but we cannot. But I can offer you an aisle seat on a flight between Chicago and the western suburbs. For $1,500.*

It should be noted that most calls to airline frequent flyer desks occur only after a passenger inadvertently clicked "purchase" on the airline's website and then realized he had bought a ticket to Damascus, Syria, (airport code DAM), when he really wanted to travel to Dallas' Love Field, (airport code DAL). Airlines have made it easier than ever for consumers to purchase tickets via websites, thereby avoiding human interaction. This can lead to major problems, as evidenced on September

12, 2013 when, due to an online glitch, fares for most domestic flights on United's website dropped to zero, save for a few paltry taxes and fees. Customers lucky enough to be surfing the site realized their family of four could now fly to Hawaii for ten dollars. Sensing a public relations catastrophe, United announced it would honor the fares. The mistake was corrected and, I assume, somebody was fired; those types of errors don't normally come with a, "let's not let that happen again," reprimand from the VP of Human Resources.

However, I have no doubt the employee at fault was able to spin the mistake into a positive experience at his or her next job interview, a trait that is becoming more commonplace in the business world. Politicians do it all the time. Former New York governor Eliot Spitzer ably convinced CNN executives that his dalliances with pricey prostitutes qualified him to be a talk show host.

I consider myself a people person.
Fantastic. You're hired!

All the ex-United employee had to do was Google "most commonly asked job interview questions" and prepare responses accordingly.

So I see you are looking for a position in our IT department?

Correct.

Your resume says you worked for many years in the—wait a minute, here it is—the 'travel industry.' Why did you leave your last job?

It was just a difference of opinion over web bookings. I thought the online ticket buying process should be a joyful experience. Upper management disagreed.

Do you have references?

Of course. Dozens of individuals praised my work. I will get you their names as soon as they return from Oahu.

What do you feel was your biggest accomplishment in your last job?

I was definitely responsible for an increase in web traffic. I was told that, on one day in particular, it spiked by about 500 percent!

Very impressive. What new ideas could you bring to the IT department?

I've been working on a new keyboard design. Today's keyboards need larger keys to reduce typing errors. And maybe some specially labeled keys like, 'DO NOT TOUCH THIS,' 'HANDS OFF,' that sort of thing.

What's the one thing you do better than anybody else?

I'm calm in the face of chaos. For example, suppose there was a bug in the system that was costing the company money. Instead of freaking out, I'd ask, 'Is this oversight benefiting consumers?' If the answer is 'yes,' I'd encourage our company to reach out to those consumers and say, 'See what happens when you do business with us? Why would you even consider our competitors?'

And did you ever have reason to do that at your last job?

Yes, particularly on my last day.

You make an interesting point, simply because the job you are interviewing for comes with a very high level of responsibility. You would be overseeing a global computer system. The slightest hiccup—even for a second—could plunge entire countries into chaos, result in emergency meetings of the world's political leaders and even alter history. Can you handle that?

Absolutely.

I believe you can. Welcome to the New York Stock Exchange.

I am often asked what drives me to obtain Executive Platinum status year after year. "What do you really get out of it?" my neighbor asked one afternoon as he saw me loading my luggage for an upcoming trip containing a typical "San Diego via New York City" route. "I mean, it's not like you're getting there any faster."

He has a point. But, we mileage chasers realize it's *how* we get there that keeps us flying via the theory that the shortest distance between two points is not necessarily a straight line, but rather an oval, trapezoid, or nonagon, depending on how many miles we need to accrue. It is why we fly to Thailand carrying nothing more than an iPad and breath mints, (why pack anything else? We're not staying). Like a fraternity of cops, the only ones who understand us are fellow road warriors, who upon hearing of our upcoming Thailand flight, will helpfully say, "If you route yourself through Ho Chi Minh City, Vietnam, you can pick up an additional 540 miles. That's what I did last year."

Should we encounter another member of frequent flyer royalty *aboard* the plane we bond immediately, sharing our lust for mileage as if we are recounting a favorite sexual experience. Or a disease.

I've had it for three years running. And I don't want to give it up.

I know what you're saying. Once you've done it, it's hard to imagine living without it.

To my pessimistic neighbor, I explain the occasional complimentary upgrade to first class, the extra legroom and the inflight meal which, although it's about the size of something consumed by your average Barbie doll, is far more nutritious then the bag of Cheetos being rationed by the family of five flying coach.

There's also the number one perk of boarding ahead of the casual traveler, a process that becomes more complicated, and cutthroat, each year. Frequent fliers, in their haste to get to their familiar home in the sky, have no issue with elbowing other passengers as they stroll down the jet bridge, never mind that those passengers are walker-assisted grandmas, infants in strollers, and Make-A-Wish recipients on their way to Disney World. All of this is perfectly acceptable to the airlines providing the elbow-swinging passenger can prove he has accrued at least 50,000 miles.

Once aboard we continue our selfish ways. While others are searching for available overhead space, we are munching on complimentary salted nuts while ordering our first of many alcoholic beverages. While others are cramming business bags beneath the forward seats, we have already removed our shoes and claimed the between seat armrest as ours.

My wife is my biggest airline status proponent. "You need to be comfortable," she will say. Translation? "You need to continue receiving those first class upgrade certificates in the mail, which I intercept and then use when my girlfriends and I go to Vegas."

Airlines, meanwhile, feed our addiction by offering other ways to accrue miles, often without leaving the ground. Need a quick 20,000? Just spend $40,000 using your airline rewards credit card. Rent a certain brand of car, stay exclusively in a single hotel chain, shop at this store, and watch the miles add up. If educating our kids in an inner city, gang ridden public elementary school came with the promise of 10,000 reward points, we'd enroll them in a heartbeat.

Frequent fliers whose jobs require international travel aren't normally sweating it out at year's end for there is always that upcoming trip to China that will push them over the edge. However, domestic travelers like myself know that a year's worth of trips to South Carolina and back aren't going to allow us to swing our elbows as we maneuver our way through the boarding line. So we must get a little creative.

Luckily, my wife is constantly on the lookout for promotions that will get me to the finish line. One year, realizing I was going to be 25,000 miles short if we didn't act quickly, she noticed a promotion in which I would earn DOUBLE miles by flying between Chicago and either Los Angeles or San Francisco.

"You just have to do three round trips to California and you'll make it," she said. "How does this sound? Chicago to Los Angeles, Los Angeles to Chicago and Chicago back to Los Angeles."

"And then I'll be done?"

"No, that's only the first day. You spend the night in LA, get up, and go LA to Chicago, back to LA and then back to Chicago."

"And then?"

"Then you're done."

"What if I want to get out of the airport and actually *see* Los Angeles?"

"The promotion ends Tuesday."

So that's what I did, flying to the Golden State, getting off to stretch my legs and turning around, often on the same airplane. With the same crew. This lead to some interesting looks from flight attendants who regarded me as a homeless person, albeit one holding a seat assignment."

Another year I was woefully short. American wasn't helping as there were no promotions to be had. I was faced with the realization of spending the next calendar year being elbowed, as opposed to throwing elbows in the check in line, when my wife proposed an outrageous idea."

"Sydney."

"Who's she?"

"Sydney, Australia," she said. "If you fly there and back, you'll make it. Providing you first fly to Houston on the way to LA before going to Sydney."

Christopher Columbus' route to the New World wasn't this confusing.

VIII

Finding Maximum Productivity in a Mini-Fridge

TO: Greg Schwem

SUBJECT: Your request

Dear Mr. Schwem:

We have received your request to install a treadmill in your hotel room during your upcoming two-night stay with us. And, in spite of your insistence that you need the treadmill because you don't want to work out with a bunch of "overcaffeinated business travelers who insist they will burn more calories if they text message while using the StairMaster," we must respectfully decline. We have a state-of-the-art workout facility on premises, containing exercise equipment with historical ramifications, meaning it was purchased in the 1800s. As long as your tetanus shot is up to date, you should be immune to any rust-borne diseases that could arise from touching the equipment. Also, we stringently enforce the 30-minute rule limit so you should not have to wait more than four hours to use the machines. If this is not sufficient, we suggest *you tie a towel to your room door handle and do some stretching exercises. If there is any other way we can be of assistance, do not hesitate to contact us.*

Sincerely,

Hotel management

Okay, this email exchange did not actually occur, but I do know that requesting a large piece of exercise equipment in a hotel room is not unheard of. Several years ago I stayed at Bally's in Las Vegas; my room was not ready for check in because, as the front desk clerk pointed out, the previous night's guest had been none other than Arnold Schwarzenegger and, "we're removing the treadmill now." Of course at the time, the treadmill's recipient was, "Worldwide movie star/budding national politician/married to a real live Kennedy Arnold Schwarzenegger," as opposed to, "Got caught sleeping with housekeeper/washed up actor/divorced Arnold Schwarzenegger." Today Arnold's request for in-room gym equipment would probably be met with a text message containing directions to a YMCA.

However, that doesn't mean there isn't a business traveler in Portland, about to take an overnight trip to Seattle, who is currently composing a letter to hotel management demanding an outrageous amenity. That's because, just as we now expect any food establishment to make us *precisely* what we order—I'm talking to YOU Starbucks customer who demands a "Grande single shot four pumps sugar free peppermint nonfat extra hot no foam light whip stirred white mocha"—business travelers feel their every need should be catered to by hotel management. Perhaps it's because rates at business hotels have skyrocketed; paying $400 a night for what basically amounts to a prison cell with a mattress and three towels is the norm, particularly if you stay in New York City.

By my own unscientific estimates, I have easily stayed in more than 2,000 hotels. My accommodations have ranged from five star oceanfront resorts to fleabags with neon signs proclaiming, "HOURLY RATES.

FREE WI-FI!" For the record, guests paying by the hour are not typically interested in surfing the web other than to monitor the police search—featuring them as the subject—that is currently underway.

I have pulled back bedspreads to find cockroaches, checked into rooms with unflushed toilets, and discovered black, muddy substances seeping from my room's bathtub drain. The last incident occurred in New York City's *Le Parker Meridien* hotel, French for *snooty desk staff*. When I contacted the front desk and requested either a partial refund or, at the very least, a room change, the manager, in a faux French accent, said neither was possible. But, he did offer to send up a fruit plate for my inconvenience.[34]

Like hotel properties, individual rooms also vary wildly in terms of luxury and comfort. Yes, the suite with a dining room table that seats eight is a nice touch but when was the last time you invited eight people to your hotel room? For dinner? The only thing a business traveler wants is privacy which is why we all can't wait to hit the road on business, despite our lies that we would "rather be home with the kids." Making that statement means you detest a bed to yourself, a television that only you control, wrapped soaps, delicious food that can be ordered via one phone call and maids who, even if they encounter a gun next to a pool of blood in your room, will simply mop up the blood and dust the gun, rendering it free of fingerprints.[35]

There are only two incidents that can interrupt this heavenly bliss. The first is a phone call from a spouse or significant other left behind. These calls should only be answered if the business traveler is not expecting room service within the next hour, something I learned the hard way.

"Hold on, I think that's room service," I said in the midst of my wife's story recounting her day, which included seven car pool trips, one sick dog, and drive-thru burgers.

---

34   A fruit plate is always the standard compensation for any problems, whatever the nature. If a 3 a.m. fire forces underwear-clad guests to jump from their balconies into the hotel pool, all would receive complimentary pineapple boats the next morning.

35   Particularly if the guest is a "Gold" member"

(CLICK)

A more appropriate response from me when I heard the knock should have been, "Hold on, I think that's maintenance here to fix the toilet that is currently overflowing onto the carpeting. Either that or we have to evacuate…again."

The second incident business travelers must deal with when staying in their private rooms are guests in the adjoining rooms having sex. Because we are currently sitting in bed, (or at the dining room table), editing PowerPoint for tomorrow's presentation, we feel such acts are entirely inappropriate, never mind that we have all caused similar disturbances with our partners. But that's irrelevant now. The more passion we hear, the angrier we become until we have no choice but to call security or knock on the offender's door and demand they wrap up their sexual escapades immediately. Or let us watch.

The American Hotel and Lodging Association said business travelers booked 41 percent of rooms in 2013. [36] These travelers were, according to the AHLA, typically male, age 35–54, employed in professional or managerial positions, traveling alone and earning approximately $127,000 per year, the bulk of which they spent on room service and mini bar purchases. That is why the hotel industry has become increasingly cutthroat; hotel executives are constantly searching for new customer service options that will keep guests coming back and paying $7 for a Diet Coke.

If one is a frequent traveler, it doesn't take long to see these innovative methods are on full display the moment the guest reaches the first stop of the hotel…

THE FRONT DESK

Like airport boarding areas, this is where America's population realizes it is clearly incapable of forming a line. I say America because, as CNN

---

36   https://www.ahla.com/content.aspx?id=36332

footage occasionally reminds us, residents of other countries patiently cue up for hours, days, and weeks waiting for medical care, bags of rice, and other life-saving staples. Somehow their methods have failed to make it to our country, where the simple act of boarding a plane where everybody has an ASSIGNED seat creates chaos.

Hotels have taken the lead of airlines and created SPECIAL LINES for SPECIAL GUESTS who FOR SOME STRANGE REASON, THINK THEY'RE SPECIAL! The rest of us are forced to wait in a single phalanx of cranky, jet lagged individuals who eventually make their way to the desk clerk, only to be interrupted by the most hated guest in any hotel, someone I refer to as the, "I Just Have a Question," lodger. We've all been intruded upon by these people; they saunter up to the clerk, announcing their exemption from waiting in line because they "just have a question." Were this question one that could be answered in a few words or a simple hand wave, e.g. "where are the restrooms," the questioner would not feel our wrath. But the questions are normally more detailed, e.g. "Can I change the credit card that I presented when I checked in? I can? Excellent. Here's the card. Please make the switch now and do it quickly as I have a spa appointment in five minutes."

Were these people to turn around and observe the rest of the guests in line, they would realize that all are scrolling their iPhones, frantically searching for a Taser app.

In spite of what appears to be mass confusion, there is some serious customer service going on in the background. Recently, as I sat in my Orlando hotel room, futilely struggling to open a complimentary coffee packet, I spied a headline in the newspaper I had just retrieved from outside my door, (another hotel amenity—the ability to step outside your room wearing only underwear and immediately be alerted to world developments),

"HOTEL STAFF 'READS' GUESTS' NEEDS."

Curiosity piqued, I elected to forgo morning java. Instead, I began reading and discovered that Affinia, an upscale hotel chain with properties in New York and Washington, D.C., had redefined the customer service experience by hiring a "body-language expert." This announcement only strengthened my theory that if you are unemployed, simply invent a title for yourself, and corporate America will hire you. At a recent company cocktail party, I met a "Director of Continuous Improvement," "Specialty Organics Manager," and "Social Network Evangelist." Not having the slightest clue what any of these people did, I greeted each with my standard opening line: "How 'bout them Cubs?"

The Affinia body-language guru was responsible for training employees to spot guests' needs or wants simply by...LOOKING AT THEM. A guest who constantly touches his face at the reception desk, the article stated, could be anxious after a long day of meetings and require extra pampering.

Or a skin doctor. Or a psychiatrist. Or a measles booster.

Since launching its program Affinia has pinpointed several common characteristics that necessitate action or discrete calls to authorities. Among them:

» Slurred speech and slight odor of Scotch- Guest prefers a room near the ice machine.

» Carrying no suitcases- Guest just had lengthy argument with airline's lost-luggage personnel.

» Carrying more than three suitcases- Guest just had lengthy argument with wife.

» Accompanied by multiple children of different ethnicities- Guest could be Brad Pitt. You never know.

» Wearing bell-bottoms or other 1970s attire- Guest was recently released from prison.

» Trouble keeping balance while walking- Guest is hiding at least three hotel towels in carry-on garment bag.

» Angry tone and finger pointing- Guest insists he did not rent *Busty Red-Headed Cheerleaders* at 2:30 a.m.

- » Profuse sweating coupled with guilt-ridden expression- Guest eventually admits he did rent aforementioned movie and needs assurance the charge will not appear on his company expense report. (That won't sit well with the Director of Continuous Improvement.)
- » Clad only in boxer shorts- Guest stepped into hallway to retrieve complimentary newspaper without room key.
- » Gnarled fingers and bloody knuckles- Guest never was able to open the coffee packet.

The body language expert is just one example of how hotels strive to anticipate a guest's needs BEFORE actually hearing them. Technology has helped in this quest as well. I was fortunate enough to stay at the magnificent Grand Wailea hotel in Maui one summer, a business trip that involved breaking a cardinal rule of business travelers: bringing one's family.

Weeks before leaving, I called to get information about the sunrise bike tours down Mount Haleakala, as I heard this was a MUST EXCURSION when one visits Maui, meaning every visitor on the island would be doing it at precisely the same time. I wanted pricing information and a concierge to dispel my daughter's fear that biking down a mountain is equivalent to being pushed over a cliff.

The Grand Wailea, being a 40-acre, 780-room hotel, naturally had a lengthy greeting message when I dialed the toll-free number. After listening to options for room reservations, weddings, spa appointments, and in-room amenities among others, I finally heard "press eight for the concierge."

I hoped to hear a friendly voice say, "Aloha," "Mahalo," or one of those other Hawaiian greetings that tourists use ad nauseum during their vacations, usually in the wrong context.

HAWAIIAN NATIVE: Quick, a volcano has erupted and blazing lava will soon spill into the main pool!!!

HAWAIIAN TOURIST: Aloha. Mahalo. Two more Mai-Tais please!

Instead, I was treated to nine ADDITIONAL PROMPTS including an option to make dinner reservations at Humuhumunukunukuapuaa[37], which, in addition to being an unpronounceable restaurant, is a type of fish and a word that would cost *Wheel of Fortune* contestants thousands, should they need to buy a vowel.

As it so often does, my mind wandered as I drifted further into the calling prompt vortex that seemingly every service-oriented business has chosen to install. Annoyed that, after five minutes on the phone, I still was unable to talk to any concierge, I invoked His name in a frustrated mumble.

"God, help me."

"Transferring call," came the reply.

"Now THAT is some serious customer service," I thought. Could the Grand Wailea really connect me to the Almighty? Why wasn't that on the website? I gripped the phone tightly, unsure yet intrigued what the next voice would sound like. I considered putting the call on speakerphone, recording it, and selling it to whatever theologian would pay top dollar. Even better, I would call the Vatican and ask to speak directly with the Pope.

"I have something I think he'd like to hear," is all I'd say. If there was no interest, I would reply, "Mahalo" and hang up.

Instead, I was connected with the lobby concierge, the object of my original quest. As was to be expected, she was courteous, knowledgeable, and informed me that the sunrise bike tour begins at 2:30 a.m. and costs approximately $500 for a family of four.

---

37   Yes, it's spelled correctly. I rechecked it 13 times

I would have gladly waited to hear THAT information.

Even so, I hung up convinced that one or more of the following is true:

1. There is a higher being and He is listening, (PERHAPS TRUE).

2. The Grand Wailea employs state-of-the-art voice recognition technology that senses when callers are frustrated and immediately bumps them to the head of the queue, (DEFINITELY TRUE).

3. The lobby concierge IS the higher being, (DEPENDS WHO YOU ASK).

Curiosity piqued, I decided to see if other businesses had adopted the Grand Wailea's voice recognition methods. Maybe invoking His name would get me faster service at other businesses known for lengthy wait times. I dialed American Airlines. After being told to say "reservations," "flight information," "award travel," "Advantage account services," or "more options," I played what I thought was my trump card.

"God help me."

The options were repeated. No help there. Apparently He is not a frequent flyer. I dialed Comcast, the cable television powerhouse, where hold times often include a change of seasons. I hung up upon realizing that the company that controls my Internet, cable, phone system, and probably my electric can opener still does not recognize voice commands, preferring to make customers push buttons in order to find out if the repairman will arrive some time before the 22nd century.

I called the Illinois Department of Motor Vehicles. Again, "God help me" got me nowhere. However, pressing 3 did connect me with a Polish-speaking agent.

"Aloha," I said. She hung up.

That ended the experiment. Much to my chagrin, I realized the phrase, "God help me" is not ubiquitous when dealing with customer service. However, I did use it repeatedly several months later while careening down a Hawaiian mountainside on a rickety bicycle.

Once the business traveler has completed front desk business, the next stop is the...

ACTUAL ROOM

In 2014 Marriott UK asked a British TV personality, rugby star, tech guru, chef and popular online blogger to share their visions for the perfect hotel room.[38] Their suggestions included digital art, an in-room hammock and atomizer, multiple LED screens, and technology capable of projecting selfie photos on the hotel wall, as if guests really want to stare at themselves as they drift off to sleep. The suggestions were cobbled together and a prototype room was created and put on display at the Westfield London Shopping Centre. Shoppers then took turns stealing all the in-room amenities.

While hotel chains continue to develop ideas for the perfect, most technologically advanced hotel room – one that will include everything from soothing noise designed to encourage sleep, and mini bars that charge you for items you merely *thought* about purchasing – they fail to realize that business travelers truly are not a picky bunch, save for the ones demanding treadmills. Sure, we occasionally complain about mattress firmness, poor sheet and towel quality, and shower water available in only two degrees (frigid and scalding). But we'll put up with those inconveniences provided there are an ample supply of one item:

Electrical outlets.

Make no mistake, the corporate traveler loves electricity. He loves it more than his spouse, his significant other, and his children. He proves this every time he comes home from a business trip and places his cell

---

38   http://www.dailymail.co.uk/travel/travel_news/article-2810925/Travellers-reveal-amenities-dream-accommodations-including-hover-bed-hot-cold-tub-selfie-wall.html

phone in a charging dock *before* he hugs his kids.[39] Because the average business traveler carries enough electronic devices on his person to power most mid-sized nuclear reactors, a steady stream of recharging methods is imperative. We cannot function knowing our iPhone is currently at 30 percent; the hotel room therefore becomes our oasis in that we can power up our tablet, laptop, phone, digital camera, and e-reader without having to search for an unused outlet in a public space such as an airport. If you ever seek an outlet in an airport, walk the entire terminal until you find the filthiest section of floor—complete with spilled soda remnants, discarded gum, and oily skid marks left by carry-on luggage wheels. Then look down. You should encounter a business executive wearing an expensively tailored suit, seated on the floor among the debris. His phone and laptop will be plugged into the two available receptacles. You need to keep walking.

While I'm not a famous British personality and therefore was not asked to contribute to the Marriott hotel design project, might I suggest one more hotel feature: A sensor that emits a shrill alarm signaling we have left one of our multitude of chargers in the room prior to checking out. It would eliminate the hefty Fed Ex bills we pay after calling the hotel and alerting the staff that yes, there is an iPhone cord behind either the curtains, the love seat, or the toilet. I have made that call on numerous occasions and been forced to pay overnight charges that rival the cost of the device itself. On one such occasion, I was told, via a phone call made from my soon-to-be-powerless iPhone, that it would cost $85 to return my charger.

"God help me, "I replied.

"Transferring call," was the last thing I heard before the phone went dark.

---

39   Guilty as charged

IX

Some Things are Better Left in Japan

In 2014, China officially overtook the United States as the world's largest economy, according to the International Monetary Fund. This finding was based on Gross Domestic Product—the total value of goods and services produced in a country during one calendar year. (If you're keeping score China took the lead by producing $17.6 trillion in goods and services compared to the paltry U.S. total of $17.4 trillion). Americans took this news in stride, seeing the figure is adjusted for China's relatively low cost of living. And considering 30 million Chinese live in caves, that's a big adjustment.

Prior to looking over our shoulder at China, America had always looked over the other shoulder at Japan, even though we rank ahead of that country in every key economic indicator save "most packages of Ramen Noodles consumed." We even pull slightly ahead of Japan in that category when U.S. colleges are in session.

American business continues to be obsessed with Japan even though it's China we should be worried about. Perhaps it's because Americans are resigned to the fact that China will one day control the Earth and, since there is nothing we can do about it, we may as well try and steal all the cool things Japan has created, before we drop to number three on the planet. We associate Japan with quality—their cars are more dependable, their technology gizmos cooler, their sushi fresher. China, on the other hand, will always be synonymous with coal induced smog, cheap kids' toys, and the 2008 Beijing Olympics, which produced Chinese female gymnasts who won the team all-around gold medal before anybody could check their birth certificates. Had anybody done so, they would have quickly discovered that the average Chinese Olympic gymnast is seven.

We love it when we defeat Japan in anything, from business deals to the Little League World Series. In 2010, you could almost hear the executives at Ford, Chrysler, and General Motors snickering when Toyota announced a massive recall brought on by gas pedals that inexplicably stuck when depressed, causing Mom's Highlander to go from zero to 120 in three seconds.

"That would NEVER happen on an American car," the executives said. "And as soon as we get out of bankruptcy and finish laying off thousands of assembly line workers, we'll build cars even better!"

And yet we remain jealous of Japan, determined to take their best ideas and incorporate them into our business methodology. True, we still can't get past the Japanese way of presenting and accepting a business card. In Japan the custom is to accept the card with both hands, briefly read it, and place it in your expensive-looking business card holder if you are standing. If seated, place the card on the table for the meeting's duration and THEN place it in your expensive looking business card holder.

In America we share contact information by bumping cellphones together.

And yet for every "Kaizen" approach to business that we borrow— Kaizen being Japanese for "good change" and encouraging workers to eliminate waste in the business process—occasionally we steal ideas that should have been left in Japan. Karaoke for example. Not only did we steal it, but we made it infinitesimally worse by deciding it could be performed ANYWHERE including corporate teambuilding events, office Christmas parties, or outdoor hotel bars. I recently vacationed in the Florida Keys where my day consisted of lounging by a pool and listening to, simultaneously, waves lapping at the shore, happily chirping seagulls, and a margarita-addled dude from New York singing Garth Brooks' *Friends in Low Places* in the key of Q Minor. An office worker with a stellar reputation on Friday can become the company laughingstock on Monday because she chose to grab the microphone at a Saturday evening corporate retreat and sing the worst version of *Summer Nights* from *Grease* since... well, since John Travolta sang it in the original movie.

Of course the Japanese are not averse to stealing our traditions and ruining them; 33 years after Abner Doubleday invented baseball in Cooperstown, NY, American expat Horace Wilson introduced the game to Japan where it continues to be played today in stadiums that feature a smaller baseball, vendors hawking bento boxes of raw fish, and a break in the game where park employees actually *clean* the stadium. Americans could reciprocate by importing the most Japanese of sports, Sumo wrestling, to our country. Wisely we have chosen not to do so.

Sumo wrestling is an athletic pursuit dating back nearly 1500 years. The Japanese love Sumo because it is a sport based precisely on their culture. It is rich in symbolism, rich in history, and rich in honor.

None of which mean a great deal in America.

One only has to travel to Japan and experience Sumo for an hour or two, before realizing how American greed, corporate marketing, and sheer hucksterism would combine to put this sport just between roller derby and professional wrestling on the "honor chart."

First, let's clear up some misconceptions about Sumo. It's not a bunch of pony-tailed fat guys running into each other while wearing diapers, which is how most Americans, after seeing snippets of it on SportsCenter or

YouTube, would describe it. Sure the contestants are a bit "proportionally challenged" and yes, their attire looks like something that holds draperies in place, but there is so much more.

Also, Sumo is not an everyday event. I assumed that hefty Japanese men, (and trust me, you have to look hard to find them in Japan), engaged in Sumo every weekend, using it as an excuse to carouse, blow off steam, and get away from the kids. We have a similar tradition in America. It's called "golf."

No, the yearly Sumo schedule consists of six "grand tournaments," occurring in four "grand Japanese cities," with tickets costing "a grand fortune." Out of sheer luck, I happened to visit Japan during the September tournament. It took place at Ryogoku Kokugikan[40] Stadium. Bob, my best college buddy and also my host thanks to his international assignment for a large advertising firm, scored the tickets. We sat in the last row, far from the stadium's ringside seats, which are not actually seats. Instead they are red mats, arranged in groups of four, and forming what we refer to as a "private box," but without a dessert cart coming by every 20 minutes full of good ol' sporting event food like prime rib and crème brulee, both of which I could sample when I was invited to a private box at a Chicago sports arena. I didn't see the value of squatting on a mat; heck, if I wanted to squat, I would have visited the Japanese toilets, or what Americans call "a freakin' hole in the floor!"

A Sumo tournament lasts about six hours and spectators are free to come and go as they please. We arrived about four o'clock. Actually we arrived about two. We found our seats about four. Even though Bob's Japanese is excellent, he apparently missed the class that covered how to decipher *kanji* characters on seat rows.

Had we been there for the start, we would have seen the *doyo-iri*, known in Japanese as "entering the ring." The *rikishi* or "fat guys" enter wearing *kesho-mawashi* or "colorful aprons." Once all wrestlers are accounted for,

---

40   Japanese for "expensive taxi ride"

the *yokozuna* appears. The *yokozuna*, from my observation, is sort of like the football team equipment manager, meaning he probably wanted to Sumo wrestle in high school but couldn't make the team on account of his thighs weren't large enough to hide small children.

The *yokozuna* claps his hands together loudly. This is supposed to attract the attention of the gods, provided the gods have found their seats. Or maybe it's just his way of saying, "grab a beer, we're getting ready to start." Oh yes, you can drink Asahi, Suntory, or numerous other Japanese brews while watching Sumo. But you must get it yourself. You can't raise a finger, yell BEER-SAN, (Mr. Beer Man), at the top of your lungs and then pass Yen down the aisle until it reaches its destination. Kaizen may be all about process, but nobody has integrated it into the "how to pay for a beer at a sporting event" process.

Now the bouts begin although when they actually "begin" is anybody's guess. The wrestlers remove their *kesho*, leaving only their *mawashi*, which barely covers their *private parts*. I have no idea who invented the *mawashi*, but I'm certain it didn't take long.

Hey Mito, the new clothing line is complete. Should I take this scrap material to the dumpster?

How much is left?

Only about enough to fit around the waist with a little left over to barely cover the butt cheeks.

Hmmmmm.

Not only do the *rikishi* wear these garments proudly, but they do a lot of bending at the waist prior to their bouts. When this occurs, all cameras cease operation for obvious reasons.

Once the *rikishi* disrobe and enter the ring, they engage in

much symbolism. They rinse their mouths with water and wipe their bodies with paper towels to purify themselves. They throw handfuls of salt into the ring, purifying it as well. Upon deciding that the ring is pure enough, they squat and face each other in the center of the ring, similar to opposing linemen on a football field. They glare, they arch their backs, they make menacing gestures, and then…they retreat to their corners and DO IT ALL OVER! Apparently Sumo wrestlers are very picky when it comes to purity. The "drink, throw, glare, arch, repeat" routine occurs several times until, at last, the *dohyo* is as pure as a Mitt Romney family reunion.

Now the match begins. Upon the signal from the *yokozuna*, the *rikishi* run full steam into each other and then basically grope with more gusto than high school senior boys during prom. Step out of the ring or touch the ground with anything other than your feet and you lose. Most Sumo matches are over in about five seconds. There were a few bouts when one *rikishi* fell down at the moment of initial impact. Sorry, match over, you lose. Next two proportionally-challenged guys, please!

What amazed me was that, no matter how brief the match, no matter what dimwitted Sumo mistake the loser made, neither wrestler seemed upset. Nobody stomped their feet, pulled out their pony tails, kicked salt on the *yokozuna* or worse, removed their *mawashi* and threw it at the opponent. Both winner and loser bowed and exited the ring. And the audience ALWAYS cheered the outcome, even audience members who were in line getting beers and missed five bouts.

The *rikishi* in the grand tournament do this every day for two weeks, putting in workdays of up to 15 seconds if it's a real grueling match. At the tournament's end, the wrestler with the best win/loss record is awarded the Emperor's Cup, which he probably takes home, fills with Suntory, and begins training for the next tournament.

That's it. That is Sumo wrestling. And in spite of my sarcasm, it was fascinating to watch in person. I found myself marveling at the ceremony, the pageantry, the symbolism, and the bouts themselves. I didn't want the bouts to end. "No, please," I thought, "don't step out of the ring. Don't fall to one knee. I want MORE!" Why did I want more? Because I MAY

NEVER BE BACK IN JAPAN. AND I CERTAINLY DON'T WANT THIS HONORABLE SPORT BROUGHT TO AMERICA.

For argument's sake, let's pretend an astute American businessman, trained at one of America's finest business universities, and employing all the cutthroat, money-grubbing business tactics that have beset America sports, football in particular, did bring Sumo to America. Admission wouldn't be an issue for, 100 yards from the stadium's entrance, some guy would be holding up tickets, saying "who needs two?" He'd offer you grandstand seats or the coveted, "red mat," section at prices roughly two hundred percent over face value. You'd pay the outrageous prices and curse yourself for not first checking Craigslist.

Upon entering the stadium you'd be accosted by souvenir vendors, selling everything from full color Sumo programs to Sumo bath towels to Sumo chocolates. Okay, some of these souvenirs exist in Japan. For 1300 Yen, I purchased a pack of Sumo playing cards, each containing a picture of a different *rikishi*. They looked like the "most wanted" playing cards that circulated after we bombed Iraq. But, unlike Iraqi warlords, identifying a Sumo wrestler in Japan is quite easy. In a country where the average man stands about 5 foot 6 and weighs 147 pounds soaking wet, 6 foot 5, 450 pound beasts wearing fuchsia diapers tend to stand out.

Souvenirs and beers in hand, you'd make your way to your seat. Unfortunately, this being American sports, it's right behind some guy yakking on his cell phone, saying something profound like, "Hey Vinnie, guess what? I'm at Sumo. No really, I'M AT SUMO! WHADDYA MEAN, NO EFFIN WAY? YEAH, EFFIN WAY. I'm using the company tickets. Hey, I think it's about to start. I'll call you back in a few. Later."

And at that moment, Sumo does start. Everyone can tell because a blonde bombshell with fake breasts spilling from her bikini has just entered the ring. The wrestlers follow her in, each wearing colorful *kesho-mawashi* laden with corporate advertising. The Pfizer wrestler walks behind the Target wrestler, who walks behind the Home Depot wrestler, who walks behind the Valvoline guy, who looks particularly buff, causing the crowd to wonder if an off-season regimen of performance-enhancing drugs is to blame.

As they parade into the ring, they are greeted with hoots and catcalls from the audience. *Yo, Advil boy, my man Winston cigarettes is going to kick your fat ass into the next dohyo.* While the opening ceremony takes place, Vegas bookmakers closely eye contestants, occasionally whipping out their cell phones and reshuffling the betting lines.

Finally a microphone falls from the ceiling. A tuxedo-clad gentleman grabs it and yells, "LET'S GET READY TO SUUUUUUU-MO." The crowd goes wild. The first two rikishi take off their ceremonial robes, revealing their diapers. The crowd oohs and ahhs in amazement upon seeing the strategically placed location of the Preparation H logo on one rikishi's mawashi. The two rikishi begin their pre-match ritual. One rikishi verbally taunts the other rikishi, loudly saying, "Yo baby, you in my dohyo now." The other rikishi counters with, "Yeah? Yo mamma so fat, she need a mawashi for each toe." Enraged, the other rikishi picks up a handful of salt and throws it into his opponent's eyes, causing brief blindness and instant purification. Both Sumo coaches charge into the ring, along with a few fans from the ringside mats, who have been drinking Asahis and Suntorys in the parking lot since 8 a.m. The ensuing brawl prompts minimum-wage security guards to appear and, "get the situation under control," with chokeholds and illegally-obtained taser guns. Finally, the ring is purified.

The contestants enter the ring. They squat, they glare, and they await the signal from the yokozuna. They charge each other. One contestant slips and falls to his knees. Match over.

Immediately cries of, "fix, fix," permeate the arena. Empty Asahi cans litter the ring. In unison, the crowd screams, "BULLSHIT," repeatedly as the television cameras roll. While the winning rikishi struts around the ring holding up 10 fingers which means, "only 10 more bouts to go," Erin Andrews snares an exclusive interview with his opponent, who causes network sensors to frantically hit the "mute" button as he explains that his knee never touched the mat and he plans to file a protest with the National Sumo Federation. To further his point, he then lays down in the dohyo for 15 minutes, refusing to move. Eventually he rises, flips off the yokozuna, and retreats to the locker room where he ingests a handful of ephedrine and awaits his next bout.

Meanwhile, 500 miles away, a 38-year-old office worker logs onto the Internet, sees the match's results and lets out a cry of disgust because the losing wrestler was part of his Sumo fantasy team.

And that would be Sumo in America. Oh, I almost forgot. Bravo Network would hastily prepare *Queer Eye for the Sumo Guy* in which five gay men teach a wrestler the finer points of food, drink, décor and personal appearance. I can almost hear it now…

"Oh Lord, that mawashi in no way matches your eyes!"

Business Students, Find Knowledge on Top of the Rock Wall

TO: Class of 1640

FROM: Schoolmaster Nathaniel Eaton

RE: Harvard Orientation

Greetings first ever incoming freshman class at Harvard and congratulations on your acceptance and for choosing Harvard, even though, at the present time, no other colleges or universities exist in the colonies. We're it.

The chill in the colonial air can only mean one thing – more taxes have been imposed on us. No, I'm kidding. It means the Harvard faculty eagerly await your arrival. Whatever your major- ship building, tobacco growing, commercial fishing, etc. – never underestimate the value of a college degree. Our staff of professors look forward to meeting you at freshman orientation. But first please be aware of some rules and suggestions upon your arrival:

Tuition must be paid before students can begin classes. We accept coin, currency and, in special instances, bartered items including animal skins and dried fish. Please visit the Financial Aid office if you feel you qualify for this type of payment.

If you own indentured servants, please leave them at home. Remember, college is about establishing independence.

Don't forget to attend the freshmen club fair! Here at Harvard we offer a variety of organizations including Junior Blacksmiths, Future Founding Fathers, and Intramural Blind Man's Bluff. GET INVOLVED!

So now we have come to the future of the business world, one that continues to rely heavily on institutions of higher learning. Colleges, universities, technical institutes—call them whatever you want as long as the mascot can be slapped on a $65 sweatshirt while not offending Native Americans—exist solely to take our nation's youth under their wings for, at the minimum, four years, and mold them into the worldly, knowledgeable minimum wage workers they are today. Armed with degrees in everything from political science to chemistry, these hourly fast food employees eventually score jobs in their fields of major but only if, while serving lattes or gluten-free burritos, they overhear a politician or chemist saying something about needing an intern. Of course, cold hard unemployment numbers don't appear on college brochures; instead they promise naïve 18 year olds that, "Your Journey Begins Here," "Your Future is Now," "You Can Make a Difference Today," or "Our Journey and Difference Making Future is Way Better Than Theirs!"

The first institution of higher learning was indeed Harvard, although Notre Dame alumni so accustomed to being first at EVERYTHING, insist it was their school. William and Mary, the second oldest university was founded nearly 60 years after Harvard; by that time Harvard had already sent numerous graduating classes out into the world and was heavily recruiting future leaders at high school fairs.

We've heard good things about this George Washington kid.

Today, according to Wikipedia, there are more than 4,500 Title IV institutions servicing roughly 20 million students, all of them currently trying to see how many Budweisers can be poured into a beer bong simultaneously while wearing boxer shorts on their heads. These numbers continue to rise in spite of clear evidence that a college degree—or any form of advanced education for that matter— is not necessary for anything other than the chance to pay yearly alumni dues. Bill Gates left Harvard in 1974, afraid that he would never have the money to repay his student loans. Steve Jobs, Oprah Winfrey, and Mark Zuckerberg also left degree-less. Then there is the case of scientist Sir John Gurdon, who attended England's prestigious Eton Academy and was told by his science teacher that he couldn't learn simple biological facts. Gurdon recounted this story in 2012 after being named winner of the Nobel Prize. For his pioneering work in stem cell research. Gurdon also awarded himself a separate Nobel Prize in the, "I Told You So," category.

Despite these stories, most professions require some sort of higher education. Colleges begin competing for that almighty commitment when students are approximately 16. Unless, of course, said student shows some sort of athletic prowess, meaning a video of nine-year-old Seth hitting a triple in a meaningless Little League game somehow finds its way onto YouTube. Late one evening, while waiting for an online porn channel to refresh, the baseball coach from East Patahootchie State stumbles upon it. He plays it in slow motion. He plays it on auto repeat. He continues playing it on a small corner of his screen while new porn covers the remainder. "Yes, yes, yes!" the coach exclaims, for he has just simultaneously climaxed and realized Seth is exactly the player that can lift the Patahootchie State Three-Toed Sloths out of their 25-year slump. The coach zips his pants and begins bombarding Seth with texts, emails, hand written notes, new baseball equipment, and suitcases full of $100 bills, all of which are perfectly legal under revised NCAA rules. Using Google Maps, he finds Seth's home address and occasionally drives by the residence, hoping to catch a glimpse of Seth on the driveway, perfecting his curve ball. He attends a few of Seth's games, drawing little attention because, like all other Little League parents in the stands, he spends the entire game staring at his phone as opposed to the action on the field. The coach's interest abruptly ceases once Seth reaches puberty and suddenly can't make it around the diamond without tripping over second base. Unfortunately, it's too late. Seth's parents, who read all the emails and notes praising their son's skills, became convinced he would receive a full ride to whatever college he chose. That's why they immediately spent all of Seth's college savings on a backyard pool and barbecue pit. Seth and thousands of kids like him are now working the overnight shift at factories that produce sardine cans.

For those parents not fortunate enough to have a child reeking of athletic or academic proficiency, the daunting task of paying for college begins approximately 30 minutes after pregnancy is confirmed. The alcohol has long worn off and both are faced with the realization that their passionate night on that Caribbean beach will cost upwards of $150,000 or twice that, if twins were conceived. Is it any wonder that condom sales rise as fast as tuition?

Enter the financial planner, an occupation that was created about the same time commas began appearing in college tuition bills. Up until then, it was not necessary to save for college. Dad brought home a paycheck, took a third of it to the local pub and used the remaining two-thirds to put food on the table, clothes on his kids' backs, and diplomas on the wall. College was an expense, much like milk, as in, "We need to pay the milkman and the college today." Now, Dad must take most of his beloved pub money and place it into a dark abyss known as a, "college savings fund," the most popular of which is the 529 plan. The 529 is appropriately named for it represents the $529 parents are left with after their child graduates. For students headed to graduate school or other forms of continuing education, that number shrinks to $5.29.

My wife and I took our planner's advice and, indeed, started 529 plans for our kids shortly after their births. We did our best to contribute each month, watching our children's nest eggs rise and then, in the crash of 2008, fall to an amount that would barely cover lunch at your average student union. Luckily the market rebounded and, when our oldest turned 16, we plunged head first into the college search, content in the realization that we had enough socked away to provide our daughter a four year education at any online university.

Incidentally, the high cost of tuition, coupled with rapid advancements in technology, has forced many colleges to offer online degrees, meaning students can finish medical school without ever leaving their pajamas. Armed with only a laptop, they can watch lectures, hand in assignments, participate in study groups, attend online keg parties and wake up the next morning with virtual hangovers. Of course all this is for naught in the event that Wi-Fi fails but at least, 60 years later, the students won't be paying off loans with their Social Security checks.

The next step in the college selection process is to make sure your child is smart enough to actually attend college. Parents don't be alarmed if, at three years old, your son or daughter cannot read chapter books as every child develops at different paces. I watched in amazement when my first, "friend who had a kid," instructed his then 18-month-old son to "go get the BLUE book" from a nearby bookshelf. He and his wife beamed with pride as the boy did precisely as instructed. Thirteen years later, that same genius would pull a knife on his mother before being sent away to military school. His required uniform was navy blue; I'm certain he picked it out himself.

Some parents feel intelligence is garnered via private tutoring or summer family vacations spent wandering art galleries and museums as opposed to Disney World. Spend a few summer days subtly following families in Washington DC and you'll get my drift. That town is filled with parents who shuffle their kids through our nation's capital trying to explain the inner workings of government in stifling DC heat, never mind that all the kids actually want is a drinking fountain and one of those portable, battery-operated fans that also squirts water. Once, while strolling near 15th Street and Pennsylvania Avenue, I got in step behind, and began eavesdropping on, a late 40s couple squiring their son, no more than six, around the city. The parents looked very professorial in stature and, I assumed, had obtained every academic degree ever created before deciding to have a child. Of course these types of people, (and you don't have to look far in Washington DC to find them), have no idea how to actually converse with children, a deficiency made apparent as the trio passed the U.S. Treasury Department. Dad pointed to the building and told his son, "That's where U.S. fiscal policy is monitored."

Their son removed his thumb from his mouth long enough to give the building a cursory glance. Both parents seemed disappointed, as if expecting their child to say, "Oh please mom and dad, can we go inside? I want to know if the Fed is going to hold the line on interest rates this quarter. Please??"

Recently, while perusing *Men's Health* Magazine online, I stumbled across an article promising, "Five Sneaky Ways to Raise Smart Kids." Of course, this being a magazine about men's health, I first had to endure pop ups promising, "MIND BLOWING SEX," and, "HOW TO LOSE UGLY BODY FAT IN FOUR WEEKS," but eventually my web browser calmed down long enough for the article to appear.

The tips were a combination of intriguing—tell them to go climb a tree because it fosters creative thinking and problem solving skills (along with the occasional broken arm)—to logical—make them earn an honest paycheck. If, after implementing these two suggestions, your child still seems stupid, you can always try the remaining three: Offer them $20 to learn to juggle, teach them to play chess, and "praise the work, not the winning."

After completing the article, I was relieved to learn college was within their grasps for they were recipients of all five. Sort of. One daughter plays chess while the other can juggle. My youngest performs household chores for income while the other snagged a job at Bed Bath and Beyond, a store that sells everything from satin sheets to red licorice ropes. My wife and I praised the work, not the winning, by spending years yelling, "Good job!" from the bleachers even when their sports teams were being slaughtered. And both girls would eagerly climb trees if our subdivision contained one over four feet.

Still, I wanted my eldest brimming with confidence before the college selection process commenced. So one day, while sitting in a tree, I compiled my own list: FIVE EASY WAYS TO APPEAR SMARTER THAN YOU ARE. These work for adults, too, and do not require investing in juggling balls.

1. **Always carry a pencil behind your ear.** Every guy who has ever showed up at my house to do home improvement projects has one. Occasionally they will use it to perform some drywall calculations; other times it just remains resting against their temporal bone for the entire day. But I've always been amazed by what these pencil-wielding dudes can do with a drab kitchen or patio, so there must be some merit to it.

2. **Wear a USB flash drive around your neck.** Capable of holding gigabytes of data, or nothing at all, these devices come in a variety of colors so they can accessorize any outfit. More importantly, having one on your person gives the appearance that you possess important information, created by you. I always thought that if President Obama wore our nation's nuclear launch codes as neck bling, he would be taken more seriously by other world leaders.

3. **Use the word "egregious" in a sentence whenever possible.** It means "terrible" or "atrocious" so there should be plenty of opportunities to write, speak or even text it on a daily basis. Also, it's one of those words that most people have heard but can't remember the meaning of so you'll sound more intelligent by proving you can insert it at will. Try it; you will egregiously thank me later. Wait, that didn't make sense. Never mind.

4. **Get a tattoo of an inspirational, non-controversial figure.** Be careful with this one. Teens who, five years ago, chose Miley Cyrus are now kicking themselves while Googling "cheap tattoo removal" multiple times daily. Even historical icons like Mahatma Gandhi and Nelson Mandela contain baggage, so go with something safe. I suggest Derek Jeter, Peyton Manning, or Flo, the Progressive Insurance TV spokesperson.[41]

5. **Stuff a reporter's notebook in your back pocket.** Occasionally whip it out and write in it. Never let anybody see the contents, for it may contain nothing more than a grocery list. The important thing is to make it appear you are writing profound ideas. Take it a step further by recording these thoughts as voice memos on your cell phone, but make sure you do it surrounded by plenty of passersby.

Natalie, my oldest, did her part by maintaining high honor roll status and getting respectable scores on the ACT, an acronym that originally was short for, "American College Testing," but that now means, "Four hours spent in a windowless room answering multiple choice questions on topics that never come up in real life." Unable to create an acronym for that, test creators opted not to rename it.

The ACT test is comprised of five skill sets—English, math, reading, science and writing—all of which must be completed before the test taker hyperventilates or, after looking at the test, opts not to attend college. Sample questions in all categories can be found via simple Google searches should the student desire to prep for the actual exam. I strongly encourage this as it gives students a chance to strengthen their BS capabilities when faced with a writing question like this:

Educators debate extending high school to five years because of increasing demands on students from employers and colleges to participate in

---

41   A safe choice provided you haven't been screwed over by Progressive Insurance

extracurricular activities and community service in addition to having high grades. Some educators support extending high school to five years because they think students need more time to achieve all that is expected of them. Other educators do not support extending high school to five years because they think students would lose interest in school and attendance would drop in the fifth year. In your opinion, should high school be extended to five years?

Students, please remember there is no "correct" answer to the writing section, which is why it's perfectly acceptable to write, "No, because I just spent five years reading this question," before moving on to the next section.

Now, armed with proof that we did have a child of at least moderate intelligence and decent BS'ing skills, we commenced searching for a traditional university, one complete with dormitories, Greek houses, academic buildings that have stood since the early 1800s (with the same ventilation systems), and football teams full of players who, somehow, are obtaining straight A's despite having never bought books for the current semester. Our friends were doing the same; neighborhood parties that so recently involved discussions about daycare, play dates, and soccer tournaments turned into "can you top this?" contests. Jennifer got accepted into THIS university, but didn't get NEARLY the scholarship money of Damien, whose test scores were ALMOST AS HIGH as Chloe's, who is TRYING TO DECIDE between every school between Maine and New Mexico. It's during these conversations where you realize that couples you've hung out with for years are, in reality, enormous ass wipes as evidenced by their desire to insert informational tidbits about their child's academic prowess into casual conversation.

ME: Gee it looks like we may get some rain tonight.

THEM: That reminds me, did I tell you that Kristin got a 35 on her ACT?

Parents, please save your bragging for Facebook as that's why it was invented.

Next we set about determining which schools to visit. This decision is made infinitely easier if your child has the slightest idea what he or she wants to do over the next 50 years, something that 99.9999% of prospective college students cannot answer. The remaining .0001% answer, "business." Therefore, the criteria becomes big school versus small, close to home versus far away, public versus private, and rock climbing wall versus no rock climbing wall (more about that later).

Natalie was a partial help, informing us she preferred a big school within a 5-hour radius of home. Seeing that I live in the Midwest that put just about every Big 10 university into play. She also hinted that she might, just might, want to become a physical therapist. We gleaned that knowledge one night when, upon asking about her future career plans, she replied, "I dunno. Maybe something in, like, health or something?"

That was all the information Sue and I needed to load up the car and spend the summer trekking across identical farmlands in search of a large school with a physical therapy program or, at the very least, a school of Kinesiology. Brimming with pride, I imagined my daughter excelling in this field, never mind that nobody has ever been in a restaurant and said, "Look who's sitting two tables over. Isn't she that world famous kinesiologist?"

Jokes aside, I thought physical therapy seemed like a useful major; at the very least she could make a nice living treating spinal curvature that all current high school and college students will have by 2020 after spending years lugging textbooks around. Digital books have yet to permeate the educational environment, at least not that I have noticed. On a recent morning, I sipped coffee and watched her amble down the driveway to catch her ride to high school. Her backpack was slung over her right shoulder, causing her to tilt precariously in that direction. Her best friend Haley waited at the end of the drive, tipping violently to the left since she chose that shoulder for her backpack. Standing together, they looked like teenage Siamese twins who had just been separated.

That afternoon she came home and dropped her backpack on the floor, causing small dishes to shudder in our pantry. I picked up the backpack and was convinced I heard my hernia popping. Once the pain subsided, I retrieved our scale from the bathroom, simply because I wanted to answer the following question: What is the weight of a good public education?

As I reached into the bag and pulled out each book, I channeled my best ringside announcer voice. "In this corner, weighing in at 4.4 pounds, the master of mathematical mayhem, ALGEBRA AND TRIG! And in this corner, tipping the scales at 5.2 pounds, the phenom of earthly phenomenon, WORLD GEOGRAPHY AND CULTURE."

"Dad, you are totally weird."

"And in this corner..."

"Dad, there are only two people in a boxing match."

"Quiet, I'm on a roll. Weighing in at a paltry 3.65 pounds, the syllabus of all things Spanish, EN ESPANOL!"

"I'm going to Haley's to study."

"Great. Ask her how her sciatica feels today. And in this corner..."

So now that Sue and I were convinced she had chosen a reputable major, it was time to find a reputable university. First stop? The University of Iowa, known for its Midwest friendliness, its comparatively modest price tag and its ability to be surrounded, on all sides, by corn. There was no need for a map or GPS; we simply relied on directions from friends familiar with the campus who told us, "Enter Iowa and, when the corn temporarily stops, you're there."

Rather than participate in the university organized tour, we opted for Katie, a family friend and current student, to show us around the campus. These one-on-one tours are beneficial in the fact that they move faster; you are not being chauffeured around the campus in groups of 40 and therefore don't have to stop while the tour guide answers inane questions posed by overinvolved helicopter parents. "Does this school offer an app I can download to wake my child up remotely?" reigns as my personal favorite.

I always enjoyed college tours, probably because as a college student in 1980-84, I promoted the benefits of Northwestern University to numerous tour groups. The key, I quickly realized, was to loudly announce the school's academic and safety records in full earshot of parents.

"OUR CAMPUS CUMMULATIVE GPA RIVALS ANY IVY LEAGUE INSTITUTION," I'd scream so residents on the other side of Lake Michigan could hear me. "NONE OF OUR STUDENTS HAS MISSED A MULTIPLE CHOICE QUESTION SINCE 1974. AND WE ALL ANSWERED THE ACT WRITING QUESTION CORRECTLY!"

"ALSO, THE CAMPUS IS VERY SAFE," I'd continue. "I HAVE WALKED THE LENGTH OF THE CAMPUS AT 3 IN THE MORNING AND HAVE NEVER BEEN SEXUALLY ASSAULTED. AT LEAST NOT THAT I CAN RECALL."

As parents admired statues of campus leaders and squirrels bussed in to give the campus a more "natural" look, I'd pull the students aside during the tour and softly confirm what they wanted to hear.

"That bar over there on the corner never asks for ID. And the guy in room 235 of that dorm always has weed."

After saying goodbye to Katie, Natalie and I continued walking, convinced we now knew the ins and outs of the University of Iowa. After spending several hours getting lost, asking a slightly stoned frat dude for directions, and being told to "walk towards the clock tower," a landmark that dots every college campus, never mind that University of Texas student Charles Whitman used his institution's tower for sinister purposes,[42] I asked Natalie her opinion.

---

42 On August 1, 1966 Whitman shot and fatally wounded 16 students from a perch inside the University of Texas clock tower. So maybe it's best to walk AWAY from the tower when touring universities

"It's nice, I guess."

That response meant the search was far from over. From Iowa, we journeyed 90 minutes west to Iowa State, a school whose slogan is, "WE HAVE EVEN MORE CORN!" This time we chose the traditional college tour, booked online the previous month. The marvels of technology ensured that a packet with my daughter's name was waiting for us at the admissions office. Even though she had yet to commit, Natalie was now the proud owner of a personalized Iowa State notebook, pencil, and steno pad! Her father was the proud owner of a three page document explaining financial aid possibilities.

Financial aid is an intricate maze of grants, loans, and scholarships, all of which your child is eligible for if he or she is at least one sixteenth American Indian. Apparently there is a serious lack of Native Americans in U.S. institutions of higher learning, so eager are administrators to court descendants of this ethnicity. The lucrative offers, (FULL TUITION, FULL ROOM AND BOARD, A JOB AWAITS EVEN IF YOU DON'T SPEAK A WORD OF CHEROKEE!), are what prompts parents to Google their genealogy histories as they sit on folding chairs waiting for tours to begin, desperately hoping they are somehow related to anybody who fought at the Battle of Little Big Horn.

Every official college tour officially begins in an identical conference room near the admissions office, student union or library, three locations always bustling with activity so parents and students see that yes, there truly is life on this campus. A fresh faced student or recent grad bounds into the room and proclaims, in precisely 30 PowerPoint-aided minutes, their undying infatuation with the school.

"There's no place like (INSERT NAME OF SCHOOL)" they'll say. "I graduated from here, but loved the area so much that I can't see myself living anywhere else." Translation? "I still haven't found a job and, if this lousy economy doesn't pick up, I will still be giving tours when I'm 62."

During these love fests, I found that one tradition has continued since my days of showcasing Northwestern, namely the mandate to recite names of celebrities who attended, even those who dropped out, flunked out, or were expelled for launching paint filled balloons onto the school president's front porch. Famous scholars, professors, or other academic-minded grads are never mentioned; celebrities who appear nightly on *TMZ* or *Access Hollywood* are cited repeatedly. During the University of Missouri tour, a photo of almost grad Brad Pitt (he left for Hollywood one credit short of a degree, quite possibly the dumbest decision he made until agreeing to star in *Ocean's Twelve*) at a fraternity party made its way onto a PowerPoint slide. His name was invoked so often, I assumed he was the school's mascot. It's actually the tiger, which sounds far better than, "The Fighting Pitts."

Then the real tour begins. Several equally well scrubbed students appear, split the audience into small groups, and head out precisely ten seconds apart. All tour groups eventually bump into each other, allowing parents to subtly switch guides once they discover their original tour leader is majoring in Early African Rock Formation. There are promises to visit lecture halls, buildings where famous research was conducted, ("Here at Indiana University, we'll see where Alfred Kinsey asked frumpy housewives questions about oral sex!"), and study-assistance centers. But first, the guides happily exclaim, you MUST see our brand new, state-of-the-art student athletic center!

It's a little known fact, but all U.S. institutions of higher learning were recently directed, under federal law, to construct massive fitness complexes that rival anything used by Olympic athletes in training. This was necessary after studies concluded students might know that John Roberts, not Jon Hamm, is the U.S. Supreme Court chief justice if they had access to 50-meter lap pools, Stairmasters, smoothie bars, and the obligatory rock climbing wall. Until I began touring colleges, I'd only seen rock walls at health clubs and retail sporting good outlets. All feature a "climber" who has scaled about three-quarters of the structure and now, dangling 100 feet in the air, looks hopelessly confused, as if his next move will be his last and he will come crashing down onto a table of discounted women's yoga pants. I never understood how climbing a wall in the middle of Dick's Sporting Goods[43] prepares one for climbing an actual mountain; most natural rock formations don't include brightly-colored plastic footholds and a spotter below constantly yelling, "You're almost there. Don't look down! By the way, yoga pants are 50 percent off this week!"

Judging by their mandatory presence at the University of Wherever, conquering a rock wall must be a job prerequisite, unless you are Native American. After touring three universities with three identical walls, I instructed my daughter to begin climbing lessons as soon as possible, as it will undoubtedly vault her over other candidates once she enters the job market.

Miss Schwem, I see you made the Dean's Lists, served as sorority president and taught English to underprivileged kids in Guatemala. But, how are your rock climbing skills?

Excellent. Check out this selfie of me at the top of Mt. Pitt!

Wonderful. Welcome aboard. For the first three months you'll be cold calling sherpas. Keep your climbing gear handy in case you need to close a deal face to face.

Parents usually stare at the rock wall as if it were the world's hardest Sudoku puzzle, so confused are they by its presence and the realization that their tuition checks will help maintain it. Also, rugged fitness was most likely not a part of their college experience. Indeed, I remember being short of breath just running down my dorm steps to greet the mobile pizza truck. At the University of Missouri, confusion over the rock wall's existence was momentarily replaced when the guide showed us another athletic facility feature...the WAVE POOL. Natalie's eyes grew wide as she silently pondered the merits of minoring in surfing.

---

43   If ever a retailer needed to change its name, it's Dick's Sporting Goods. It would eliminate the awkward moment that ensues when somebody, upon opening a gift card from the retailer, proudly says, "Thanks, I love Dicks!"

At some point during the tour, the guides attempt to point out actual students. This is easier said than done, particularly if the tours take place during the dog days of summer. Even schools with populations exceeding 30,000 are ghost towns between June and August, emptied of everyone except students taking summer school classes, working campus jobs, or hanging around because their parents, upon receiving end of year report cards, refused to pick them up. Smaller schools often hire town residents to pose as students; if you see two men wearing t-shirts with Greek letters tossing a Frisbee in the quad, chances are they're collecting paychecks. They are also at least 50 years old.

No campus visit is complete without a dorm tour. The guides announce this as if it's a bonus, available only for you lucky participants on today's tour and only because you are in the prestigious company of me, the tour guide, and keeper of all university secret codes.

Normally they don't let outsiders into the dorms but I happen to have a key!

The guide approaches the dorm and swipes an electronic card. A buzz is heard and the group is shepherded into the dorm's lobby where, behind a desk, they see a half asleep, half hung over work-study student posing as dorm "security." While the desk attendant explains dorm entrance procedures to the enrapt parents, (One cannot enter the premises without an electronic card, an ever-changing three-digit building code and a retinal eye scan), a four-man band of burglars who joined the tour at the dorm's entrance are now stealing laptops and iPads from the top floor while the tour continues three floors below.

The group shuffles past the high-tech laundry room, (Just swipe your wash card. No cash needed!), the dorm cafeteria, (Just swipe your meal card. No cash needed!), and a few closed doors where grunting and heavy breathing are heard, (Just swipe your sex card. No cash needed!), before arriving at an empty room reeking of disinfectant and looking as if it had recently been swept by a Secret Service detail. This, the guide exclaims, is a standard room in this, our newest dorm. We aren't showing you our older dorms because rat exterminators are currently on site. The new ones, however, contain amenities that you parents might not have experienced in your dorms. For example, wall to wall carpet, air conditioning, Wi-Fi, a Starbucks on every floor, and you're reading this correctly—WEEKLY MAID SERVICE. Yes, I heard this more than once, leading me to wonder what type of person takes a job as a dorm room maid? I have stayed in hundreds of hotels and often feel guilty knowing that, upon my departure, a sweet, underpaid, hard working woman will open my door, stoop down to pick up some wet towels, and change sheets that may contain a few room service crumbs. A dorm room maid, conversely, gets the opportunity to dispose of used condoms, drug paraphernalia, and pizza crusts from previous semesters, all while vacuuming around a passed out fraternity pledge who now knows the powers of Jägermeister.

Parents and students crowd into the room, lost in their thoughts. Moms gaze at the tiny closets and small dresser drawers, convinced their children will die of pneumonia because there is not ample space for winter sweaters and coats. Meanwhile the students stare at the bunk beds, wondering if it will be possible to have sex on the top bunk while a roommate sleeps below. It's another question the tour guide will answer out of parents' earshot.[44]

Finally, the tour circles back and arrives at the dorm cafeteria, where attendees are invited to eat whatever they can consume in 45 minutes. The guides hover nearby, picking at salads or other light fare since all will probably be climbing the rock wall later that day and don't want to feel bloated.

Dorm cafeterias have also been "moderately upgraded" in the past 10 years, meaning they now contain more food than can be found on your average cruise ship. Today's college students will never know of dorm cafeterias that contained one nightly entrée that, if not comparable to one's palate, meant the student was forced to skip dinner or find enough

---

44   The answer is "yes" if you have an understanding roommate and a dorm room with a vaulted
     ceiling

loose change to order a pizza. At Northwestern, the latter decision often occurred when the cafeteria fare was a creation known as "Broccoli Cheesebake," a dish containing two main ingredients and several lesser known chemicals not included in the title.

While Broccoli Cheesebake may still exist on college dinner menus, rejecting it means the student is forced to walk ten feet to another food "station." Maybe it's the deli. Or stir fry. Or Italian. Or sushi. Or vegan! Yes parents, rest assured that your babies will now get their proper fill of vegan entrees whenever they are hungry.

Our campus tours, rock wall ogling, and cafeteria glutton fests continued all summer; the University of Wisconsin and Marquette were toured and discarded as were Iowa State, Drake University, and the University of Missouri, despite Brad Pitt's spiritual presence. Whenever we returned home, we found our mailbox stuffed with invitations to visit other schools. Most were from colleges that wouldn't exist were it not for their aggressive marketing campaigns; Stanford, for example, has yet to mail our household a "WE WANT YOU!" letter whereas other, lesser known institutions do everything short of offering to pick your child up in a limo with a police escort if that's what it takes to get them to visit. The choices overwhelmed our daughter, as evidenced when I entered her room one evening and found her sitting on her bed, awash in a sea of glossy college brochures filled with photos of smiling sorority girls, strapping football players, and freshmen chemistry students who, judging by their joyful expressions, had just eradicated all potentially fatal diseases in one afternoon.[45]

"Made a decision yet?" I asked.

"This is so hard," she said.

"Choosing a college typically is," I said. "What are the finalists?"

"Well this one," she said, holding up a green and white brochure, "says it's advancing knowledge and transforming lives."

---

45   Brad Pitt did this while at the University of Missouri. At least that's what the tour guide said.

"So let's go visit," I said, trying to be helpful. "A little knowledge advancement and life transformation never hurt anybody."

Discarding that and picking up a two-tone blue leaflet, she said, "But this one says, 'Start Here, Go Anywhere.'"

"So?"

"So if I'm transforming lives at this school, will I be able to go anywhere? Or will I be stuck in the same place?"

"Good point."

"Maybe I should consider this one," she said, picking up another brochure. "It says, 'Your Revolution Starts Here.'"

"Take that off your list," I said. "No daughter of mine is going to join a revolution."

"How about, 'Your College, Your Future?'" she said, picking up an armload of pamphlets, reciting the bold-faced taglines and dropping them on the floor one by one. "Open Minds Creating Futures?' 'Reach Within, Shape the Future?' Dad, do you think I'd be better at creating the future or shaping it?"

"Why not just join the Army?" I said. "They promise you can 'Be All You Can Be.' That ought to get you a job somewhere."

"Dad, the Army stopped using that slogan in 2001. Now it's, 'Army Strong.'"

"Okay, the Army's out," I said. "Let's get back to that 'shaping the future,' thing."

"See how hard this is?" she said.

"Honey, you're not supposed to pick a college because of a slogan or an ad tagline," I said, knowing full well her decision would probably come down to whatever school had the best wave pool. "Wherever you choose, you're going to get a good education."

"Unless I go here" she said, scooping up another brochure. This one says, 'A Foundation for Life.' Nothing about education. I could come out of there stupid after four years."

"At least you'll have a foundation," I said.

"Dad, this isn't funny. It's stressful. Plus, I don't even know if these places are going to accept me."

"Then you need to come up with your own campaign," I said. "The only purpose of college marketing slogans is to get your attention and make you wonder what you'll be missing if you go somewhere else. So, when you apply, include a slogan that makes the college want you. Make sense?"

"I can't think of any slogans."

"There are plenty of websites that will create one for you," I said. "Go to slogangenerator.org."

She pulled it up on her Mac. "Now what?"

"Imagine yourself as a product. Describe yourself."

"I'm an undecided high school senior."

I typed those words into the box and clicked, "Generate slogan."

"No, you're not. You're a 'devoted undecided high school senior maven!'" I said excitedly, even though my daughter's new description rivaled that of a LinkedIn job seeker. (See chapter 2).

"It doesn't say that," she said, looking at the screen. "Oh wait, yes it does. I'm trying something else."

I looked over her shoulder as she typed, "Smart volleyball player."

"What's it say?" I asked.

"That I'm a 'Delighting Smart Volleyball Player Enthusiast'."

"What university wouldn't want that?" I said. "I'll bet Harvard and Stanford would roll out the red carpet for you!"

"I'm smart, Dad. I'm not Harvard smart. We both know I didn't get a perfect score on my ACTs."

"Too bad," I said, taking the laptop and typing 'perfect ACT score" into the generator box. "Then you'd be a 'Savvy Perfect ACT Score Purveyor!'"

"Maybe I'll just take a year off and work at Starbucks," she sighed, pushing the brochures away and picking up her iPhone.

"You're going to college, young lady," I said. "Your mother and I didn't spend a summer staring at corn for nothing."

"Are you sure?" she said, returning to the slogan generator website. "'Wicked Starbucks Barista, Bar None' has a nice ring to it."

I sighed heavily, the sound of a "Frustrated Dad."

Or an "Experienced Frustrated Dad Artisan."

XI

The Office of the Future Will Be Very Nutritious

IN EARLY 2015, THE OFFICE CHAIR TOOK A GIANT STEP TOWARD extinction.

Already the Internet was full of studies suggesting everything from too much caffeine, to mid-morning snack breaks, to accepting a car pool ride with Kyle in accounting would hasten workers' deaths. Then, along came scientific findings from Canadian researchers saying desks could be lethal.

No, they didn't mean workers would expire from inadvertently cracking their craniums on open desk drawers; nor did they predict a rise in electrocutions due to punching computer monitors. Instead, they focused on the chair, concluding that too much "sedentary time," Canadian-science speak for "sitting on your butt" elevates the risk for cancer, cardiovascular disease, Type 2 diabetes, and the most obvious affliction…hemorrhoids.

I find it ironic that Canadians came to this conclusion, considering I sit for inordinately long periods every time I visit the country. Most of this sitting occurs in a Canadian Customs holding area, across the desk from somebody with a badge and an inflated sense of importance. The badge-wearer stares me up and down, glances suspiciously at my passport, returns his distrusting gaze to me and then casually asks me if I have, "ever had any trouble getting into Canada," as if that information is not flashing across his screen underneath my photo. In Fall 1995, lacking a Human Resources and Skills Development Canada exemption—and not realizing one might be necessary to serve as narrator for a Canadian telecom company's tradeshow presentation—I was abruptly stopped, sent back to the US and told not to return to the country for one year. Canadians, as I found out, do not take kindly to foreigners entering their borders to perform skills they think they can perform themselves. Exceptions are made only for those who can talk freely about hockey.

On that day in 1995, I sat in the holding area, alongside unclaimed luggage and one vicious looking dog, for a good eight hours. Attempts to stand up and stretch my legs were met with reprimands and, in one case, a physical threat. Despite the hostile treatment, I have returned to Canada at least a dozen times since that unfortunate day and, despite having to go left at the first Customs checkpoint while everybody else heads right towards the exit, I've managed to enter the country using one of three explanations:

» I am here for "pleasure" and not "business" (even though I find little pleasure in visiting a country that gives me the "Al Qaeda" treatment)

» I am a performance artist and will only be here for a limited time (the truth and what I failed to say in 1995)

» I am Santa Claus (This only works if I choose to enter Canada on Christmas Eve)

Around the same time as the "sitting is deadly" study hit the press, the Rietveld Architecture-Art-Affordances (RAAAF), a Dutch studio that operates "at the crossroads of architecture, art, and science"[46] decided

---

46   http://www.raaaf.nl/en/

it had the solution to the derriere dilemma: Eliminate chairs in the workspace altogether.

It makes perfect sense that such an idea would come from the art world simply because you rarely see anyone sitting down to view art, unless that person has been dragged unwillingly to an art gallery and spends the day texting from a bench, not realizing the bench is made of priceless, Italian Renaissance-era marble and part of an exhibit entitled, "The Furniture of Michelangelo." (The velvet ropes surrounding the bench should have been a tipoff). This is why I never touch anything in museums, even restroom hand driers, for fear that I am unknowingly desecrating a masterpiece. Even famous artists washed and dried their hands, right?

The RAAAF installation, dubbed "The End of Sitting," looked a bit like a 3D puzzle that had yet to be completed; similar to one of those *Survivor* challenges where contestants must assemble a puzzle after swimming 50 yards while holding a canvas bag between their third and fourth toes. Each time we watch that strangely enduring show, my wife says, "How long do you think you'd last on the island?" I reply that, upon landing, I would immediately recuse myself from the game and ask for a job with the production crew…you know, the ones who leave the island every night and stay at a luxury hotel with a pristine balcony overlooking the ocean. The balcony is close enough to the *Survivor* island, so the crew can watch the contestants eating bug larvae while they gorge themselves on all you can eat breakfast buffets.

"The End of Sitting" featured a hodgepodge of pieces, separated by nooks and crannies so narrow that it would be impossible to actually sit between them, unless you worked for a company that employed toddlers. Workers could only stand, lean or, in some cases, lie down while conducting office work. The design also looked as if it would make a great setting for a spirited office after hour's game of "Hide n Seek."

The idea immediately took root; RAAAF even fielded inquiries asking if it was accepting orders though the office was merely a prototype. But it advanced the already-percolating conversation on the future of chairs in the company office. Naturally, making employees healthier by eliminating chairs met with resistance from company "wellness experts" whose jobs could potentially be eliminated. Right now they are tasked with making employees healthier by snooping in employee desk drawers after hours and removing all Gummi Bears.

Designing a more productive office environment is on the minds of everyone from CEOs to entry level employees. In 2013, Yahoo CEO Marissa Mayer rocked her company's morale by ordering a portion of the workforce – mostly customer service reps – to return to the office. No more working from home, she said. The employees begrudgingly made the switch and, as of this writing, still do not have cable since they are no longer able to wait at home for the cable repairman.

Some companies, most notably Google, offer cafeterias and vending machines stocked with free food. In other cases, it's free eggs, as in human eggs. Apple and Facebook are among the companies that offer to freeze female workers' eggs gratis—occasionally even letting the women stop working while the egg retrieval procedure takes place! The rationale behind this precursor to in vitro fertilization is that healthy eggs will be available if the career driven female chooses to put off child bearing until later in life. Unfortunately for men, sperm freezing has yet to be offered. So guys, don't show up for a job interview in Silicon Valley carrying a brown paper bag and casually ask where you can store it in the event you are hired.

Complimentary yogurt pretzels and egg storage aside, most of the discussions on future offices revolve around physical appearance, transparency, and how both will improve employee collaboration and productivity. Reception areas, once viewed as the drawbridge to the castle, with the receptionists serving as sentries, now are viewed as concealing the brains of the operation. "What are you hiding?" office designers ask. "Why not let visitors immediately see that actual work is taking place?"

This suggestion was immediately rejected by receptionists nationwide who argued that playing solitaire while simultaneously updating an iTunes playlist is, in fact, "working."

Transitioning to the office of the future will no doubt be tricky and time consuming as many companies are reluctant to spend money on what they currently have, specifically a non-descript floor of cubicles; the cubicles ringed by individual offices occupied by longtime employees who smugly glance out at the cubicle workers. Sections of the floor or, in some cases, entire floors, are broken down into individual departments, all headed by an assortment of vice presidents who coolly refer to themselves as "VP" whenever they get a chance, even if it's in the waiting room at the local Jiffy Lube. [47] The VP's also refer to themselves as "upper management," blindly unaware that there is no such thing as, "lower management," and therefore, their titles are unimpressive. And whether the company has five employees or 5,000, all contain the obligatory personnel:

» IT Director – Knows exactly what the company's product does, but can only describe it via a combination of PowerPoint slides and flow charts. Incapable of formulating words.

» VP of Marketing – Has no idea what the product does, but man, can make it sound awesome!

» VP of Sales – From the golf course, constantly sending emails to IT and Marketing asking what the product does.

» Director of Human Resources – Forever wanting to pull the product from production, fearful that it might offend certain ethnic groups. Not solely responsible for firing people, but considers it a wonderful job perk.

» CEO – Can't explain the product, has no idea what it does and doesn't care who it offends.

» Recently laid off employee – Knows exactly what the product does, can clearly explain it, and had sketched out many ideas on cocktail

---

47   Telling a Canadian customs official you are VP of comedy is useless

napkins demonstrating how the next version could be even better. (CHECK IN THE EX-EMPLOYEE'S DESK DRAWER. THE NAPKINS ARE LOCATED NEXT TO THE GUMMI BEARS.)

Face it, every office worker fantasizes about changing the environment where a third of a 168-hour week is spent. Sadly many of those fantasies are rife with violence and include removing the CEO, either through the front door or, in extreme cases, out an 25th-floor ergonomically designed window created by a famous Italian Renaissance-era artist. In order for America to remain in lockstep with other world powers in terms of productivity and the race to create the world's first robot that will inevitably replace ALL office workers, I feel a change is needed at the top. In spite of the Tea Party's insistence that government should keep its nose out of everything except the annual White House Easter Egg hunt, I feel Washington should step in and create a new cabinet position: Secretary of The Grind, devoted to improving the office employee's daily work experience. This position will be entirely separate from the Secretary of Labor. While that position is supposed to look out for workers nationwide, it also must look out for retirees who are currently bombarding the department with angry letters wondering why their pension checks have yet to arrive. Answering those letters requires seven eighths of the labor secretary's time so he really needs some help.

The Secretary of the Grind would be tasked with tearing up the current business environment and starting from scratch. I nominate myself for the position even though I have never worked in an office. But I did work in a newsroom, which resembles an office in the fact that the same people show up every morning and spend the rest of the day screaming at one another.

Once nominated by the President and confirmed by Congress, a process that will certainly hasten my death since I'll most likely be sitting for months while Congress makes a decision, I will place the following recommendations on the president's desk:

All office buildings and company headquarters would be moved out of cities and densely populated areas and into states with plenty of open space. Iowa would replace New York City as the nation's business capital with Montana and Kansas close behind. Wall Street would cease to exist as the Stock Exchange, Board of Trade, Mercantile Exchange, and other financial institutions would relocate to Ottumwa, Iowa. Meanwhile, Wall Street would be rezoned residential, with condominiums and townhouses available only to those who participated in Occupy Wall Street. At last they could claim victory!

Office complexes would exist side by side with farms so farmers would have somebody to talk to other than their wives and cows. The farmers would partner with surrounding businesses by supplying crops for office workers. Instead of running to Taco Bell or McDonald's for lunch, workers need only go to the break room, where enormous bags of fresh green beans, carrots, celery, and lettuce await. Onions and radishes would be forbidden for obvious reasons. Fridays would be deemed, "Ranch Dressing Day." In return for contributing to a healthier workforce by donating vegetables, farmers would get free technical support since an IT manager would always be nearby. The vegetable spread would also eliminate the number one criminal offense plaguing corporate America: Breakroom refrigerator theft![48]

Company titles must contain at least two words and those words must rhyme. One need only look to the success of the Piggly Wiggly grocery store chain to see that this is a fabulous idea. Also, coming up with a rhyming name would foster creativity among the company's founders; those who couldn't come up with a suitable name would call on rap musician and rhymer extraordinaire Eminem, who could produce several options in seconds. I've never been a huge fan of Eminem, but marvel at his ability to slip phrases like "Munchausen's Syndrome" into a verse:

---

48 Insider trading is a close second

"Goin through public housing systems

Victim of Munchausen's Syndrome.

My whole life I was made to believe I was sick when I wasn't" – Cleanin' out My Closet.

Xerox would have to find another name as no company could place an "x' in its title. This would ensure that we never returned to the confusing 1990s when tech startups like Xircom dotted the business landscape, manufacturing xonfusing products that nobody could xigure out.

All offices would be inaccessible via public transportation and carpooling would be forbidden. Every employee would arrive via separate vehicle, thereby ridding the workforce of employees who infect the entire office with flu germs acquired from a subway passenger with post-nasal drip. Opponents will cry that my plan will lead to massive road congestion. I'll counter by saying I have NEVER seen a traffic jam in Iowa, Kansas, or Montana.

Work shifts would contain no set hours; employees could come and go as they pleased as long as all worked eight hour days. I'd be happy with an 8 a.m.-noon shift, followed by 2-3 p.m., and then 7-10 p.m. The office would only contain single people and childless workers between 2:30 and 4 p.m. as the rest of the workers would be meeting their children at bus stops and asking how their days went. The latchkey would return to being something that unlocks a door and never again equated with a child who comes home to an empty house, an unsupervised television, an Internet-enabled PC, and a pantry full of cookies.

Still, I would encourage early arrival by creating parking spots chock with fringe benefits. Those who arrived in predawn hours would be treated to spots close to the office, with cement that heats in the winter months and is refreshingly cool in the steamy summertime. Each spot also contains a machine brewing complimentary Starbucks and an attendant who watches over your car until it's time to leave. Parking spaces further from the office go down in desirability; tardy employees will be forced to park in spots that always contain discarded fast food bags and a layer of black ice, even in summer.

All company receptionists would be chimpanzees who high five workers as they pass into the office's inner sanctum. The chimp is also charged with patting down every visitor–male and female–before they enter. Should the chimp find weapons on a potentially disgruntled customer or ex-employee planning to do harm, he is trained to wrap his arms around the visitor's neck and repeatedly French kiss him until the weapon-toting individual runs screaming from the office. The parking space attendants, all retired security officials, would take it from there.

Newly hired employees will be announced via loudspeaker and will enter the office to thunderous applause from the current, (and already standing), workforce. My theory is that everybody deserves the feeling of being recognized before they have actually done anything. As a comedian, I receive this feeling every time I enter the stage. It's nice.

Every office will be circular or hemispherical in shape and contain all the architectural traits of a "whispering gallery" where every conversation will be heard by everyone else in the room, despite an employee's best attempt to use that low, "don't repeat this to anybody; it's just between you and me," office voice so common in today's workplace. Famous whispering galleries can be found in London's St. Paul Cathedral, Chicago's Museum of Science and Industry, and, allegedly, in front of the Oyster Bar in New York City's Grand Central Terminal even though nobody ever whispers in New York. My design will eliminate office gossip.

All offices will have a dress code: Speedo bathing suits for men and Spanx for women. Unflattering clothing such as this will encourage employees to look one another in the eye, a practice that all but disappeared with the onset of text messaging. At precisely 8:30 a.m. all employees – everyone from mailroom attendants to senior level marketing executives – will be required to engage in some form of group exercise. Every Wednesday is

Boxing Day. All employees will receive gloves on their first day, but they are filled with air and don't cause physical pain when they connect with an opponent's face. However, anyone not bringing boxing gloves to the office will be required to fight with their bare hands, against an opponent of my choosing, and I'll always choose Sergei from shipping. Such a handicap will improve employee retention; day planners will no longer be needed as slow-to-heal bruises will serve as reminders that Wednesday is fast approaching Exercise on other days might include Pilates, square dancing, or jumping onto a Velcro wall wearing a Velcro suit.

Computers and the company local area network will not be switched on until 9 a.m. Employees arriving before that time should meditate or, if it's Wednesday, shadowbox in preparation for their upcoming bouts. Any visitor to the company's website before 9 a.m. will be redirected to a site featuring nothing but YouTube clips featuring puppies licking infants in bouncy chairs. They will be so entranced they will quickly agree to purchase whatever product the company manufacturers, no questions asked. The economy will prosper.

Conference rooms will become extinct after my department uncovers proof that nothing was ever achieved on a conference call. The lone exception occurred in 1993, when a four person sales team from Xingxang successfully made a tee time at Pebble Beach, only to have to nearly cancel it hours before tee off because one of the team members had a conflict; he had to take a mandatory conference call. Other team members encouraged him to do it while they played golf, a move that resulted in the foursome being ejected from the course after other golfers complained about the rude guy with a cell phone yelling, "Who just joined?" on the fourth green.

Every office will employ a "Flash Mob" consultant who comes in once a month and trains the entire office to spontaneously twerk. Every company will be required to have a summer picnic and office Christmas party. Children will be welcomed at both. The picnic won't feature tug of war, sack races, or any other competitions that will cause hard feelings and backstabbing on Monday morning as employees eat their vegetables; instead all picnic-goers will participate in a communal project for an impoverished country. Entertainment will be provided by whomever is the nation's hottest country singer at the time. Employees can drink as much beer as they want; it will be non-alcoholic, but everyone will think it's high in alcohol simply because it will have one of those strange microbrew names like Sister Barley's Sweetwater Ale. Some employees will act drunk even if they're not.

Christmas parties will be void of "Secret Santa" gifts, employees fighting over who should wear the Kris Kringle outfit this year and DJ's who set up their equipment in the reception area. Christmas bonuses will go away, eliminating angst and disappointment. Everybody, regardless of performance, receives an identical raise the first of the year. Higher performing employees receive sealed envelopes labeled, "To be opened after your death." Inside relatives will find stock options and use of a condo in Hawaii for one week. The pain of losing a loved one will dissipate.

The spell check feature would be eliminated from all office computers. In its place every office would employ a retired copy editor from either the *Washington Post* or *New Republic* magazine who would proofread all sales proposals, PowerPoint presentations, and interoffice memos and verbally abuse any employee guilty of misspelling or improper punctuation. Several shocked employees would wander over and ask the proofreader to please keep his voice down, a request rendered moot due to the whispering gallery feature.

All employees would get four weeks' vacation, which must be used in a calendar year. No fair banking vacation days for two years and then going on a 10-week African safari/Wailing Wall journey during the company's busiest season. Stock options as part of a company hiring package will disappear as that will eliminate the desire to constantly refresh a stock ticker screen and rejoice, or agonize over the fact that, on Wednesday, the stock moved a tenth of a percent.

I would institute one mandatory, "Take Your Daughter/Son to Work," Day. However, instead of sitting next to their parents' desks, Snapchatting and appearing hopelessly bored, the kids would receive an eight hour class courtesy of the copy editor who would scream at the kids until they finally learned the difference between "your" and "you're."

Once a year, a team of consultants would arrive, thinking they have been hired to make the company run more efficiently. Upon their arrival, all would be shot with rubber dart guns given to every employee until they run screaming from the building. The chimp would high five and French kiss each on their way out.

The following words and phrases would be stricken from everybody's vocabulary: reorg, think out of the box, paradigm shift, stick to our knitting, grab the low hanging fruit, win win, push the envelope, robust, rich set of tools, proactive, impactful, 800-pound gorilla (the chimpanzee/receptionist finds that one especially offensive), out of pocket, circle back, doing more with less, user focused, thought leader, boots on the ground, hit the ground running, get off the ground, perfect storm, game changer, eco-centric, and seamless integration. Anyone caught using these words would be relegated to fighting Sergei for the next four Wednesdays.

I would employ a top team of scientists and computer programmers to invent, for real, the neuralyzer contraption from the *Men in Black* films, which immediately erases memories. The device would be used on employees who quit the organization, but have sinister plans to steal the company's trade secrets and customer lists.

All offices will be locked on weekends; any employees caught lurking around the premises hoping to put in some "extra work" will be blindfolded, thrown into the back of a van and driven directly home or to their children's weekend activities.

Corporations would be forbidden from advertising at professional sporting events. From now on, football team captains participate in the coin toss, not the Chevy Malibu coin toss. Baseball players hit home runs, not Menard's round trippers, and basketball players will no longer shoot from the GoDaddy three-point arc. Corporate box seats at stadiums will disappear, eliminating fans who attend games only because they "have the company seats."

Finally, business schools and business degrees would disappear. Every third grader would be required to take one eight week business class, taught at a third grade level. Any student who shows promise would begin a corporate internship immediately.

It might be the only way to get kids to eat their vegetables.

CPSIA information can be obtained at www.ICGtesting.com
Printed in the USA
LVOW10s0300220915

455176LV00002B/3/P